Hugh Cameron Gillies, Alexander Stewart

The Elements of Gaelic Grammar

Hugh Cameron Gillies, Alexander Stewart
The Elements of Gaelic Grammar
ISBN/EAN: 9783743347724
Manufactured in Europe, USA, Canada, Australia, Japa
Cover: Foto ©ninafisch / pixelio.de

Manufactured and distributed by brebook publishing software (www.brebook.com)

Hugh Cameron Gillies, Alexander Stewart

The Elements of Gaelic Grammar

THE ELEMENTS OF GAELIC GRAMMAR

BASED ON THE WORK OF THE

REV. ALEXANDER STEWART, D.D.

BY

H. CAMERON GILLIES, M.D.

LONDON

PUBLISHED BY DAVID NUTT

270-271 STRAND

1896

Edinburgh: T. and A. CONSTABLE, Printers to Her Majesty

THE ELEMENTS OF
GAELIC GRAMMAR

OTHER WORKS BY H. CAMERON GILLIES, M.D.

THE THEORY AND PRACTICE OF COUNTER-IRRITATION

Price 6s. *nett.*

'A valuable addition to the small number of books which are of practical use to surgeon and physician alike.'—*Medical Times.*

'Dr. Gillies is to be congratulated on his courage in producing such a work.'—*Provincial Medical Journal.*

'Certainly well worth reading by all who take a wide and philosophical view of the problems presented to them in their daily work.'—*The Hospital.*

'The profession owes a debt of gratitude to Dr. Gillies for his effort to place the widely used, and abused, practice of Counter-Irritation on a rational basis.'—*Edinburgh Medical Journal.*

THE INTERPRETATION OF DISEASE

Part I. The Meaning of Pain. Price 1s. *nett.*
 ,, II. The Lessons of Acute Disease. Price 1s. *nett.*
 ,, III. Rest. (*In preparation.*) Price 1s. *nett.*

'His treatise abounds in common sense.'—*British Medical Journal.*

'There is evidence that the author is a man who has not only read good books but has the power of thinking for himself, and of expressing the result of thought and reading in clear, strong prose. His subject is an interesting one, and full of difficulties both to the man of science and the moralist.'—*National Observer.*

'The busy practitioner will find a good deal of thought for his quiet moments in this work.'—*The Hospital Gazette.*

'Treated in an extremely able manner.'—*The Bookman.*

'The attempt of a clear and original mind to explain and profit by the lessons of Disease.'—*The Hospital.*

CONTENTS

PART I

OF PRONUNCIATION AND ORTHOGRAPHY

CHAP.		PAGE
I.	OF LETTERS :—	
	The Alphabet,	1
	The Sounds of the Vowels,	4
	The Powers of the Consonants,	9
II.	ASPIRATION OF THE INITIAL CONSONANT,	11
III.	ECLIPSIS AND VOWEL CORRESPONDENCE,	17

PART II

OF THE PARTS OF SPEECH

I.	OF THE ARTICLE,	21
II.	OF NOUNS :—	
	Gender,	27
	Declension,	35
III.	OF THE ADJECTIVE :—	
	Declension,	54
	Aspiration,	60
	Compound Words,	61
	Comparison,	63
IV.	OF NUMERALS,	67
V.	OF PRONOUNS,	73
VI.	OF VERBS,	83
	Formation of Tenses,	87
	Verb IS,	90
	Particles,	91
	Verb BI,	99
	Is with BI,	101
	Regular Verb BUAIL,	102
	Irregular Verbs,	108
	Auxiliary Verbs,	112

CHAP.		PAGE
VII. OF ADVERBS,		116
VIII. OF PREPOSITIONS,		119
	Prepositional Pronouns,	137
	Compound Prepositions,	142
IX. OF CONJUNCTIONS,		146
X. OF INTERJECTIONS,		149

PART III

OF DERIVATION AND COMPOSITION

I. OF DERIVATION,	150
II. OF COMPOSITION,	152

PART IV

OF SYNTAX

I. OF THE SENTENCE,		154
II. OF CONCORD :—		
	Article and Noun,	156
	Adjective and Noun,	159
	Pronoun and Antecedent,	162
	Verb and its Nominative,	164
	Agreement of one Noun with another,	166
III. OF GOVERNMENT :—		
	Nouns,	169
	Adjectives,	170
	Verbs,	171
	Prepositions,	172
IDIOMATIC CONSTRUCTION,		173
NOTE ON REGULAR VERB WITH PARTICLES,		175

PREFACE

THE purpose of this Grammar is to afford assistance to such as may desire a living and intelligent acquaintance with the Gaelic language of Scotland. With this object in view, it was at first my settled intention to make little or no reference to the older language, but I soon found this to be impossible. An intelligent understanding of the Gaelic of the present day cannot be attained without some reference to the older language from which the later Grammatical forms had origin. There is no pretence to learning in these pages, nor any attempt even to indicate the results of modern Gaelic scholarship. I have admitted nothing which I did not believe would be helpful to the elementary student; and I hope my references will be found correct, and my inferences also correct and useful.

I have the advantage of being in touch with intelligent students of the language as their teacher, and I have made their actual difficulties guide me in everything. I hope I have been able in some degree to enlighten and to smooth their way, and that of others also who may undertake the same most interesting travel.

I followed the plan of Dr. Stewart's Grammar as closely as possible, feeling that I could not hope to improve upon it. I have also appropriated all of his work that I possibly could, even to his very words. Dr. O'Donovan—no mean authority—declared Stewart's Grammar to have been 'by far the most important work on Gaelic that ever appeared'; and I cannot express my admiration of it as I should wish. No one can ever clearly see or fully know the philosophical comprehensiveness and the artistic unity of this work, but one whose duty compels him to weigh and examine every word and line as I had to do. All that I claim is to have extended a little way into the light of to-day, the lines which Stewart laid down so well; and all I hope is that I have done so consistently and in some measure worthily.

I endeavoured to have special regard to the phonetic basis of the language and have always appealed to it whenever it was necessary to do so. It is from the speech-power of the organs of Voice that all speech-form proceeds. The written language is at best but an approximation to the spoken word, and the sense of Hearing comes as a not very stable or reliable medium between the Voice and the written Character. The principle of Aspiration which plays so important a part in Gaelic Grammar is based on phonetic expediency, so is Eclipsis, and so the Vowel law of Correspondence. No attention given to this aspect of the language is lost; without attention to it the language cannot be understood. But as my reference can only be partial and occasional I should wish all who may desire to know this aspect of Gaelic Grammar to refer to Mr. Mac-

Farlane's very useful work on *The Phonetics of the Gaelic Language*.

The division of Nouns into three Declensions is different from all previous classifications. My departure from Stewart's philosophical arrangement I wish to justify by the explanation following:

The method I worked upon was by Exclusion.

1. The great class of Abstract Nouns in **achd**, and those in **e** and **ad** of Comparative forms, which have no inflection, were thrown out.

2. Such Nouns as are indeclinable in the Singular—all Nouns ending in a Vowel—were next taken as the First Declension.

3. Of Nouns ending in a Consonant it was found that a great number had a distinct inflection forming a Genitive in **i**. This class was made the Second Declension. It always has the characteristic Vowel Broad.

4. Nouns ending in a Consonant and having a Small Vowel characteristic were made the Third Declension.

But it was found that a considerable number of Nouns remained, which though ending in a Consonant and having a Broad characteristic, were not declined in the Singular. This class must form a Fourth Declension or be included in the First. I have preferred the latter alternative as being the more simple way.

Regarding this classification it is to be remarked that Nouns of the Second Declension are so peculiarly distinct from all others, that they must form a class by themselves. There can be no question regarding them.

It may be said that the First and Third might be put

under one Declension inasmuch as they have no inflection of the Singular—excepting those of the First that make the Genitive in a, and those few of the Third that make it in e. The fact however that all of the one class must be 'exceptions' to the other, if they are put under one Declension, appears to me sufficient reason, even if it was the only reason, for classing them separately. The difference in the inflection of Adjectives of the one class and the other decides the matter conclusively in favour of two Declensions.

I have satisfied myself, by actual working results and otherwise, that for the purpose of learning Gaelic the arrangement of Declensions which I have given is the simplest that is possible. The arrangement according to Original Stems, even if they were clearly determined is, I am convinced, impracticable. To begin with they were far from regular, and they have so changed from their first form that it would be a desperate task for the beginner to master, first, the Original forms, and then their extremely involved later changes, before he approached the living tongue which he wishes to learn; and all this labour is the less necessary because, whether for good or for evil, the tendency of the language in its later development has been towards that uniformity which I have endeavoured to present.

The arrangement of the Tenses of the Verb is so far new. It has order and simplicity in its favour, and it discovers a point of supremely logical correctness—that there is no Indefinite Present Tense in the language. If linguists had not neglected to examine the Gaelic tongue, to their own great loss and disadvantage, there would not have been such confusion to them about the Aorist in other languages; and there would have been scarcely sufficient reason for so great ado over 'the lucid and remarkable discovery,' made so late in the day, that the forms used and taught as Present Tenses in Latin and Greek are not such at all but Imperfect Progressive or Aorist Tenses. The English can say *I strike*, an Indefinite Present form, and we thought that *verbero* and τύπτω were identical with it in meaning and it was made a point against Gaelic that its poverty was so manifest that it had lost, or never had, a form for the Present Tense. But now, we find that at any time it could have supplied all the light necessary to a 'lucid and remarkable' correction of languages and teaching of the highest respectability; and we find that what was too eagerly seized upon as to its discredit is only one other proof of its superiority.

Whatever errors in the accepted forms of the written language I had occasion to point out, I have not ventured to make any change. I have deferred to custom throughout, even in some things which I am sure have nothing to commend them, but which I hope an intelligent common consent will soon rectify.

I intended to have given some Lists of Parts of Speech at the end, but have thought it better to give these in a small book of carefully graduated Exercises running parallel with the order of the Grammar, which is in hand and will soon follow.

Almost all my references to the older forms of the

language are taken from Zeuss's *Grammatica Celtica*, Stokes's *Kalendar of Oengus*, and Windisch's *Texte*.

I am very much indebted to my Publisher, at whose expenses this book is issued; and I hope that all to whom the Gaelic language and tradition is more than a mere curiosity or patriotic fiction will appreciate Mr. Nutt's practical services, as they are bound to acknowledge the scholarly diligence and enthusiasm with which he has investigated very important chapters of the Gaelic life-story.

I could have no greater pleasure or satisfaction than to know that I had done something to commend my native Gaelic tongue, to which I owe so much of all I esteem most valuable, but I fear that my fragmentary and infrequent leisure for Gaelic study has not been conducive to good work. It may however stimulate others, with more opportunity and greater competence, to do better and in that way serve my ultimate purpose.

4th April **1896**.

THE
ELEMENTS OF GAELIC GRAMMAR

THE Grammar of the Gaelic language may be conveniently studied in four principal divisions or parts, treating :—

    I. OF PRONUNCIATION AND ORTHOGRAPHY.
    II. OF THE PARTS OF SPEECH.
    III. OF DERIVATION AND COMPOSITION.
    IV. OF SYNTAX.

PART I—OF PRONUNCIATION AND ORTHOGRAPHY

CHAPTER I—OF LETTERS

THE Gaelic Alphabet consists of eighteen letters, **a, b, c, d, e, f, g, h, i, l, m, n, o, p, r, s, t, u.** Of these five are Vowels, **a, e, i, o, u**; and the rest are Consonants.

For the purposes of Grammar, the Vowels are divided into Broad, **a, o, u**, and Small, **e, i**.

Of the Consonants, **l, n, r**, and **s** sometimes, are called Liquid Consonants, and all the rest Mute Consonants.

Mute Consonants may be divided, according as they are mainly produced at the lips, at the teeth, or at the throat, into Labials, **m, b, p**, and **f**; Dentals, **d, t,** and **s** sometimes; Gutturals, **g** and **c**; and these may be classed, according to the force with which they are produced, as Weak, Medium, or Strong. For example, the Labials, **m, b, p,** are in their order the Weak, Medium, and Strong Consonants of that class.

Though a Weak Dental or a Weak Guttural does not appear in the Alphabet, there can be no doubt that these occur in speech. The Welsh language, indeed, has **ng** as a single character in the Alphabet; **fy ngalar** *my grief*; and **n** is a mutation of **d**, as in **dwrn** *a fist*, **fy nwrn** *my fist*. It is important to know and to recognise this, for it greatly simplifies some interesting points of Gaelic Grammar. The Weak Dental is an **n**, and the Weak Guttural is also **n**, but a little attention will show that these are produced at entirely different parts of the organs of speech —that, indeed, the one is a Dental and the other a Guttural **n**. The one stands related to **d** and **t**, and the other to **g** and **c**, as **m** is seen to be related to **b** and **p**. Mute Consonants may therefore be conveniently stated as follows:—

	WEAK.	MEDIUM.	STRONG.	
Labials,	m	b	p,	and f
Dentals,	(n)	d	t,	and s
Gutturals,	(n)	g	c	

For convenience Medium and Strong Consonants will be referred to by the usual terms of *Mediae* and *Tenues*.

Liquid Consonants have been called also Semi-vowels, because they partake of the character of Vowels as well as of Consonants. Their usage will illustrate this. They are commonly met with after Mute Consonants at the beginning of words and syllables, and before Mutes at the end, forming a transition from Consonant to Vowel and from Vowel to Consonant—as **clann, cnoc, crann**; and **olc, ponc, cearc.**

N is not a frequent nor an acceptable Liquid at the beginning of words. It occurs with the Labials, only once with **m** (in the cases of **bean** *a woman*), and only once with the Dentals (in **tnù** *envy*). With Gutturals it occurs a few times, as **cnò, gnè**, etc. But in every case in which it is used it is almost, if not quite, pronounced as **r**. At the end of words it comes freely before the Dentals and Gutturals—to which it rightly belongs.

S is placed among the Liquids, not because it is in itself a characteristic liquid letter, but because its grammatical conduct in certain positions is that of a Liquid. When **s** is followed by a Mute, its conduct is quite different from that of **s** followed by a Vowel or by a Liquid Consonant, as may be seen in the agreement of the Article and Noun, where the Nominative of the Feminine, the Genitive of the Masculine, and the Dative of both Genders are aspirated and take **t** before **s**-initial, while Nouns in which initial **s** is followed by a Mute do not aspirate, but behave like Nouns that have a Dental initial. **S** in the latter position may, for convenience, be called **s**-mute; and in the other, though the expression is not quite correct, it may be called **s**-pure.

The Aspirate **h** is not used as a Radical Consonant.

Of the Sounds of the Vowels

The Vowels **a, i, u,** represent one simple sound each; **o** and **e** represent two sounds; and the combination **ao**, which will be studied as equivalent to a single Vowel, has two sounds.

This statement is not strictly correct, as it will be presently seen that **a, o,** and **u** represent other sounds also, but it is made for the sake of simplicity, and these other sounds of **a, o, u,** are, and with perhaps more propriety, referred to in another connection.

All Vowel sounds may be long or short.

A long Vowel is often marked with an accent, especially when the quantity of the Vowel determines the meaning of the word; as, **bas** *the palm of the hand*, **bàs** *death*, **lon** *greed*, **lòn** *a meadow*, **caraid** *a friend*, **càraid** *a pair*, **tur** *quite*, **tùr** *a tower*.

The Accents are two, Grave and Acute; as, **è** *he*, **cé** *the earth*.

The Grave Accent may be used on any Vowel, but the Acute on **o** and **e** only; as, **àrd** *high*, **sè** *he*, **cìr** *a comb*, **òr** *gold*, **ùr** *new*, **té** *a female*, **bó** *a cow*.

For convenience, advantage will be taken of these two Accents to indicate and distinguish the two *qualities* of the sounds of **o** and **e**, as well as mere accentuation. Thus, **ò** will indicate not only an accented **o**, but also and always an *o* of the same quality as that in English *lord*; and **ó** will represent the long *o* in *tone*. So **è** will be for the sound of *e* in *there*, and **é** for that in French *fête* or *a* in English *fate*.

The following statement indicates the simple sounds of the language as nearly as they can be represented by English equivalents.

	AS IN ENGLISH.	LONG.	SHORT.
A	far, fat,	{ **làmh**, *a hand* **màl**, *rent*	**dag**, *a pistol* **glas**, *a lock*
È	there, met,	{ **gnè**, *kind* (of) **cè**, *cream*	**deth**, *of him*
É	féte, date,	{ **cé**, *the earth* **té**, *a female*	**leth**, *a half* **teth**, *hot*

There are only a few words in modern Gaelic in which these sounds are represented by **e** alone. The **è** sound is most commonly represented by **ea** and **eu**, and the **é** sound by **ea**, **eu**, **ei**, and **ai**, thus:—

	LONG.	SHORT.
ea = è	{ **neamh**, *heaven* **seamh**, *peaceful*	**fear**, *a man* **bean**, *a woman*
eu = è	{ **neul**, *a cloud* **meud**, *magnitude*	
ea = é		{ **eas**, *a waterfall* **fead**, *a whistle*
eu = é	{ **teud**, **ceum**, *step*	
ei = é	{ **féill**, *a market* **céir**, *wax*	**meidh**, *a balance* **geilt**, *cowardice*
ai = é		**mairbh**, *the dead* **tairbh**, *bulls*

	AS IN ENGLISH.		
I	see, feet,	{ **cìr**, *a comb* **tìr**, *land*	**mil**, *honey* **dris**, *a bramble*
	io = i	{ **iomhaigh**, *an image* **ciobair**, *a shepherd*	**iodhal**, *an idol* **biodag**, *a dirk*

	AS IN ENGLISH.	LONG.	SHORT.
ò	lord, sort	bròg, *a shoe* lòn, *a meadow*	sop, *a straw* cnoc, *a hill*
o	tone, bone	bó, *a cow* fóghnan, *a thistle*	crodh, *cattle* gob, *a beak*
ù	poor, put	cù, *a dog* lùb, *a twist*	rud, *a thing* ugh, *an egg*

Ao is not a Diphthong but a simple sound, of which, like **e** and **o**, there are two distinct qualities, one like *u* in English *cur*, but lengthened, and one very nearly like *u* in *sun*.

For convenience let these sounds be represented by û and ū.

	AS IN ENGLISH.	LONG.	SHORT.
û	cur (lengthened)	aol, *lime* gaol, *love*	
ū	sun (lengthened)	aonta, *a lease* naomh, *a saint*	laoidh, *a hymn* saoi, *a hero*

The first of these sounds, û, is also represented sometimes by **a, o,** and **u.**

	LONG.	SHORT.
a = û	adhradh, *worship*	lagh, *law* agh, *a heifer*
o = û	foghlum, *knowledge*	foinne, *a wart.*
u = û		cuthach, *madness*

When two simple vowel sounds are pronounced continuously and as one, the sound is called a DIPHTHONG.

It has already been seen that two vowel characters may, and do very frequently, come together, without forming a Diphthong. This should be carefully observed.

The following are the Diphthongs of Gaelic:—

	LONG.	SHORT.
ai	{ cainnt, *speech* { saill, *fat*	
èi	sgeimh, *of comeliness*	sgeimh, *of disgust*
éi	geinn, *a wedge*	{ deigh, *ice* { feidh, *ease*
òi	doimhne, *the deep*	goimh, *anguish*
ùi	Goill, *Lowlanders*	goil, *a boiling*
ūi	{ cuibhle, *a wheel* { suigheag, *a raspberry*	cuip, *a whip* muime, *a stepmother*
eò	ceol, *music*	
eó	leomhan, *a lion*	meomhair, *memory*
ia	{ bian, *a skin* { gniomh, *a deed*	
iû	{ biadh, *food* { cioch, *a teat*	
iu	{ cliu, *fame* { iongnadh, *wonder*	iubhar, *the yew-tree* piuthar, *a sister*
ua	{ duan, *a poem, canto* { snuadh, *complexion*	
uû	{ cluas, *an ear* { fuath, *hatred*	
iū		ionnas gu, *so that*

THE TRIPHTHONGS of Gaelic, if there are indeed any, are few. Perhaps the combination **uai, eòi**, in such words as **fuaim, geoidh** are, or are near to being, Triphthongs; but they are the only combinations called

Triphthongs which can be by any right so named. The combinations usually classed as Triphthongs are either Diphthongs or single sounds; thus:—

  aoi as in **caoidh** = ūi a diphthong.
  eoi ,, **deoir** = èò   ,,
  iai ,, **flaire** = iû   ,,
  iui ,, **ciuil** = iu   ,,
  uai ,, **gluais** = uû   ,,
  aoi ,, **caoin** = û a single sound.

The use of the last i in these combinations is to indicate that the Consonant following is to be pronounced Small. Similarly the use of **e** in **deoir** is to give the Small sound to the preceding **d**. This is the use always of silent Vowels.

The sounds hitherto referred to are those of the Accented Syllable. The sounds of Unaccented Syllables are always short and simple, and are frequently obscure or uncertain.

The sound **a**-short is met with in the Prefixes **an, ana, as, ath**; in the Diminutive Suffixes, **an, ag, eag**; and in the Adjective Suffix **ar**.

The sound **è**-short is that in the Diminutives **ean, ein**; in **ear, air, ein, eid, aid**, denoting an agent; in the Abstract Termination **eis**; and in the Adjective Terminations **ail, eil**.

When **i** is alone in an unaccented syllable, the sound is simple **i**-short; but when **a** or **u** precedes it, a shade of **û** comes into the sound.

Ò-short occurs in the Adjective Termination **mhor, or**.

Ù is the sound of **a** and of **e** final, as well as in the Abstract Terminations **achd, ad, ead, as, eas, adh**, in the Adjective Suffix **da**, and in the verbal endings **am, amaid, adh, tar, ta, te**.

Of the Powers of the Consonants

The Mute Consonants, when in initial positions, are pronounced as in English, but distinctly stronger and sharper or clearer, and they have a more outward or forward movement in expression; as compare :—

	ENGLISH.		ENGLISH.
bog *soft*	bog	**port** *a harbour*	port
dos *a bush*	doss	**tom** *a hill*	Tom
gas *a twig*	gas	**cas** *a foot*	cash

All Consonants are affected by the Vowels that precede, flank, or follow them, giving them the character of Broad and Small, as :—

ad	**bid**	**madadh**	**idir**	**dàn**	**deoch**
a hat	*a chirp*	*a dog*	*at all*	*a poem*	*a drink*

in which the influence of the Vowels on **d** may be observed.

The Mediae **g, b, d**, in final positions and at the end of syllables, are quite as strong as the Tenues in English; and the Tenues **c, p, t**, in similar positions, have a peculiar asperation of the last part of the sound approaching them.

Mediae—**gob**   **trod**   **dag**   **luban**
　　　　　a beak　*a scolding*　*a pistol*　*a puddle*
　　　　　　　　　　bradan　　**lagan**
　　　　　　　　　　a salmon　　*a hollow*

Tenues—**bac** = bahc　　**cnap** = cnahp　　**cat** = caht.
　　　　　　a ledge　　　　*a lump*　　　　　*a cat*
So **acair** = ahcair　**capul** = cahpul　**cnatan** = cnahtan
　　an anchor　　　　*a mare*　　　　　　*a cold*

All Consonants may take the Aspirate, except **s**-mute; but with the Liquids **l, n, r** it is not expressed. The Aspirated Consonants have the following powers:—

mh and **bh**, = *v*, and **ph** = *f*.
dh (with small vowel), = *y*, and **th** is a strong breathing.
gh „ „ = *y*, and **ch** is a strong Guttural.
sh = *h*.

Though **dh** and **gh**, affected by Small Vowels, are very near to the English power of *y*, when affected by Broad Vowels they approach to the power of a soft Broad **g**. Compare **bidh** *of food*, **brigh** *substance*, **dhith** *of her*; **ghillean** *of lads*, with **dhath** *of colours*, **ghath** *of arrows*, **buadhan** *virtues*, **stuadhan** *billows*.

Mh and **bh** after a Broad Vowel and followed by a Liquid Consonant, have the power of English *w* in *now*; **samhla** *likeness*, **samhradh** *summer*, **cabhruich** *sowens*, **cabhsair** *a causeway*. **Mh** and **n** are sometimes silent; as in **comhla** *together*, **manran** *crooning*, the preceding vowel having a nasal tone.

Fh is silent, except in the initial of the words **rhathast** *yet*, **fhein** *self*, and **fhuair** *found*, in which it has the power of **h**.

The Liquids **l, n, r** are as in English, but fuller and stronger, and enunciated farther forward in the mouth. These are the only letters that may occur double; and when **ll, nn** do so occur after Broad Vowels at the end of words, they reflect a peculiar influence on the preceding Vowel, making it end in a *w* modification of the sound; **dall** *blind*, **toll** *a hole*, **fann** *weak*, **tonn** *a wave*.

CHAPTER II—ASPIRATION OF THE INITIAL CONSONANT

ASPIRATION is the name given to the influence on a Consonant of an *h* immediately following it; as, **duine** *a man* **a dhuine** *O man*, **ceann** *a head* **a cheann** *his head*, **piob** *a pipe* **mo phiob** *my pipe*.

Liquid Consonants do not show aspiration in writing, though the influence of aspiration is easily perceived in the spoken language when the Consonants are in aspirable positions. Compare the pronunciation of the following phrases:—

Not Aspirated.		*Aspirated.*	
a lamh	*her hand*	**a lamh**	*his hand*
an nighean	*the daughter*	**mo nighean**	*my daughter*
an reachd	*the law*	**do reachd**	*thy law*

Initial **l, n, r**, in aspirated positions, are pronounced exactly as if they were followed by **h**; and it has been frequently suggested that the **h** should be written in such positions, or that some indication equivalent to it should be made, such as doubling the letter, or placing a point over the Consonant, as is done in Irish. This would certainly be an advantage to learners; and it is simply a question of expediency which method should be adopted. The custom of Scottish Gaelic, however, is not to indicate the aspiration of Liquids, and that custom will be deferred to in this work. If it is remembered that these aspirate in all positions in which Mute Consonants do, any difficulty arising from this seeming defect may be easily overcome.

Aspiration in Gaelic has been represented by some grammarians as in effect similar to the Asperation of Greek grammar, where the roughening of the initial is brought about by the introduction of a strong breathing, which has been taken to be equivalent to English *h*, as may be seen in the borrowed words *rhetoric* and *rhomb*. This view is wrong, and greatly misleading. The Aspiration of the Consonant in Gaelic is a softening, and the very opposite of the Greek roughening.

That the purpose of Aspiration in Gaelic is to soften the Consonant is well shown by the initial change which the Adjective undergoes when joined to a Feminine Noun. It is—

tarbh crosda	*an angry bull.*	but	**bó chrosda**	*an angry cow.*
fear pòsda	*a married man.*	„	**bean phòsda**	*a married woman.*
each trom	*a heavy horse.*	„	**lair throm**	*a heavy mare.*

In all these the softening is evident, and it is so always. The Mediae show it even better; **tarbh geal** *a white bull*, **bó gheal** *a white cow*, **fear bàn** *a fair man*, **bean bhàn** *a fair woman*, **fear dàn** *a bold man*, **bean dhàn** *a bold woman*.

Most interesting confirmation of this view is to be found in the changes of the Feminine Adjective in Welsh, which, though it softens, does not do so by Aspiration, or at any rate not always. The Welsh has—

ceiliog coch	*a red cock.*	**iâr goch**	*a red hen.*
tarw penwyn	{ *a white-headed bull.*	**buwch benwen**	{ *a white-headed cow.*
ceffyl trwm	{ *a heavy horse.*	**caseg drom**	{ *a heavy mare.*

So **ceiliog gwan** *feeble*, but **iar wan**; **tarw byr** *short*, but **buwch mher**; **ceffyl da** *good*, but **caseg dda**. The **w** of Welsh is like long *ó*, and **dd** is like a very soft English *th*.

When a word is aspirated, it is said to be aspirated by the word preceding it; as, **ceann** *a head* **mo cheann** *my head*; **cas** *a foot*, **do chas** *thy foot*, where **ceann** and **cas** are said to be aspirated by **mo** and **do**. This is usually taken to mean that **mo** and **do**, and such words as end in a Vowel sound, need a smooth approach to the succeeding initial Consonant, which is therefore aspirated—that is, smoothed down. Though this is true to a great extent, and is the most comprehensive principle underlying Aspiration, it does not always hold true, and it is not in every case an accurate expression of the grammatical facts. Final vowels are not always followed by Aspiration. In many cases the second word influences the first as much as the first does the second; and in a great many cases and conditions the rule does not hold in any way. It will be puzzling to the learner why **a** *his* should aspirate, while **a** *her* does not. It will also be observed that when, for instance, the Noun after the Article is aspirated, the Article itself loses the final **n**; there is thus a smoothing down, not only of the initial Consonant, but also of the terminal Consonant of the preceding word—a mutual accommodation to make the movement from the one to the other easier. That this is the intention there can be no doubt, for where it is not necessary it is not used, as when the Article is followed by Dentals, which are easy to approach from the final **n**; as, **ceann an duine** *the head of the man*, **ceann tighe** *the head of a house*. Initial Labials, again, when not aspirated, determine a change of the Article to **am**, for the same reason of making the movement easy.

Thus it may be seen that it is not quite correct to say that the one word aspirates the following word, for they interact in somewhat similar degree; but when the first word ends in a vowel, the second may, without impropriety, be said to be aspirated by it. For convenience however, the ordinary form of expression may be used, so long as the meaning of it is understood.

Aspiration occurs in the following circumstances:—

1. The Vocative Case of Nouns, Singular and Plural, is always aspirated.

2. One Noun governs a succeeding Noun in the Genitive, and aspirates it in the Genitive Plural; as, **cean circe** *the head of a hen*, **cinn chearc** *the heads of hens*.

Masculine Proper Nouns are aspirated in the Genitive Singular; **baile Dhuneidin** *the city of Edinburgh*, **cas Dhomhnuill** *Donald's foot*.

Compound Nouns formed of Noun and Noun, or of Adjective and Noun (p. 61), have the second element aspirated in all the Cases.

3. The Article aspirates the Noun following in the Nominative of the Feminine, the Genitive of the Masculine, and the Dative of both genders—in the Singular (p. 23).

4. A Noun aspirates a succeeding Adjective as follows:—

All Masculine Nouns aspirate the Genitive Singular of the Adjective, and Masculine Nouns of the Second Declension aspirate the Nominative and Dative Plural also (p. 60).

Feminine Nouns aspirate the Nominative and Dative Singular, but never the Plural.

When the Article precedes the Noun, the Adjective following is aspirated in the same cases as it is aspirated by the Noun alone, and in the Dative Singular Masculine besides (p. 60).

In Compound Adjectives the second element is aspirated throughout (p. 62).

5. Of Cardinal Numerals **aon** *one* and **da** *two* aspirate the Noun following, but **aon** does not aspirate initial Dentals **d, t, s**, for reasons which have been given. The word **ceud** *a hundred* is aspirated by the first four numerals. These aspirate alone, and in their recurring combinations with **deug**, for *ten*; as **aon fhear** *one man*, **da fhear** *two men*, **aon fhear deug** *eleven men*, **da fhear dheug ar fhichead** *thirty-two men*.

Of Ordinal Numerals, only one causes aspiration **an ceud** *the first*; **an ceud fhear** *the first man*, **a cheud bhean** *the first woman*.

An t-aona is the form in which this (*the first*) combines with **deug**, but it does not cause aspiration. It is **an aona** for Feminine Nouns.

6. The Personal Pronouns are aspirated as follows:—

Mi after **bu** and **cha** in the tenses of the Verb **Is**.

Tu, when Nominative to a Verb, is always aspirated—except with **Is**, and in the Future Indicative and the two tenses of the Subjunctive Active.

The unaspirated form is never used with the Passive forms of the Verb. The Accusative form is always **thu**.

The Possessives **mo** *my*, **do** *thy*, and **a** *his*, aspirate the Noun following. **A** *her* does not aspirate; and Whitley Stokes says this is because in its old form it ended in **s**, as it does in Sanskrit **asya** *his*, **asyas** *hers*. The Plurals of Possessives do not cause aspiration.

7. Verbs of the regular declension have an initial Consonant aspirated in the Past Tense of all Moods, Active and Passive; but the Past Subjunctive, Active and Passive, does not aspirate after **mur, nach, gu'n, na'n**.

The Future Subjunctive is aspirated in the Active and Passive, and the Future Negative after **cha**.

The Verb **bi** is aspirated like the Regular Verb.

8. The syllables **ro, glé**, and **fior**, used as Intensive Adverbs, cause aspiration of the Adjective following.

9. Prepositions which end in a Vowel, or of which the old forms ended in a Vowel, cause aspiration of the succeeding Noun.

10. The Conjunctions **ged, ma, o**, cause aspiration of the initial Consonant of the Verb following: **ged thuit mi** *though I fell*, **ma thig mi** *if I come*, **o'n thainig mi** *since I came*. See 'Particles' (p. 91).

Generally, when an initial Consonant is aspirated, it indicates that the preceding word ends, or at some past time did end, in a Vowel sound.

A Dental sequence usually prevents Aspiration.

CHAPTER III—ECLIPSIS

THIS is the name given to a grammatical expedient, still used in Irish Gaelic though not in Scottish Gaelic, which aims at fluency by appearing to facilitate the pronunciation of an initial Consonant when it is a *tenuis* or a *media*. This is done by placing the weaker Consonant of the same class before the stronger, as a sort of stepping-stone; thus, **ar bpéin** *our punishment*, **ar mbaile** *our town*, **ar dteine** *our fire*, **ar ndia** *our God*, **ar gceart** *our right*, **ar ngearan** *our complaint*.

The custom now is not to pronounce the root Consonant but only the eclipsing one; as, **ar béin, ar maile, ar deine**, etc. This is not a desirable result.

The name Eclipsis which implies that something is obscured or cut out of the word is not correct, for there is nothing cut out. The real meaning that underlies this expedient does not appear to be understood even by Irish grammarians. It seems to be primarily an attempt to represent the process through which the organs of speech go in order to produce the Consonants, and is closely analogous to the use of Diphthongs and Triphthongs as these are used for the fuller indication of the character of vocal sound. The *tenuis* **p**, for instance, cannot be produced by the organs without passing through the position at which **b** is produced, and **b** cannot be approached but from the simple contact of the lips which we have named **m**. There is thus an essential organic sequence of **m, b, p** so close that the three might without much impropriety be looked upon as one letter or one organic result. It is so also with **n, d, t** and **n, g, c**.

This explains why **n** and **m** were the eclipsing letters of the old language—it could not be otherwise. It suggests also that the eclipsing final **n** which is said to be now 'drawn' towards the initial of the following word is a mistake of the grammarians, against which Nature has prevailed. The language used to be written, as it was and is now spoken, in phrases, and in breaking these up no little violence has been done to word forms: **leisantorc**, for instance, which we make **leis-an-torc**, perverts the Preposition and the Noun, and destroys the Article. It should be **le-sant-orc**. Perhaps eclipsing **n** is only 'drawn' to its proper place in such phrases as **ar ndia, ar ngearan**.

The meaning of Eclipsis will now be comparatively clear. It will be observed that in every instance the eclipsing letter and the eclipsed, form part of one or other of the three essential sequences shown. But the Irish does not appear to be quite consistent in its methods. As we see, **p** is eclipsed by **b**, and **b** itself when initial is eclipsed by **m**. Why it may be asked if it is necessary to eclipse **b** when it is in an initial radical position, why is it not necessary to eclipse it when in an initial eclipsing position? This is manifestly inconsistent. If the principle were carried out properly we should have such forms as, **ar mbpein, ar ndteine, ar ngceart**; and this is actually how it used to be. In the Catechism of 1725 we meet with **a ngcumhachd** *in power* (Q. 6), **gu saorsa a ndtoile fein** *to the freedom of their own will* (13), **a mbpeacadh** *the sin* (15).

It will be observed also that whether Eclipsis is or is not indicated in the written language it is an essential feature of the spoken language, in Scottish Gaelic as truly as in Irish. It becomes an interesting question therefore whether it should or should not be indicated in writing. Reason would appear to be on the side of the Scottish method of not indicating Eclipsis. If the strong Consonant contains the *media* and the weak of the same class, and if the *media* in the same sense contains the weak, *and if it cannot be otherwise*, there would not appear to be any need that the fact should be indicated. There can be no doubt that the indication in writing of this process entails a considerable loss of time and trouble; and it certainly disfigures the language and obscures its etymology. That any advantage comes by it is not apparent.

Such forms as **an t-slat** *the rod*, **an t-socair** *the ease* have been demonstrated as the remains of a general system of Eclipsis in Scottish Gaelic, but this is an error. These forms are not an Eclipsis nor in any way akin to it. The **t** in such cases results from the phonetic hardening of the **d** of the Feminine Article **ind** before aspirated s-pure, which always happens.

It is interesting to notice that Eclipsis and Aspiration are as two linguistic inclined planes, the one inclined or rather acclined *upwards towards* the *tenuis* and the other declined *downwards from* the high position. Since neither term Eclipsis or Aspiration is correctly expressive of the intention in the expedients which they name, the terms Acclination and Declination might with advantage take their place.

An extremely helpful and perhaps philosophical way is to consider speech and to study it as one continuous sound of which the Vowels are but so many characteristic portions chosen at certain points for convenience to illustrate the whole, and the Consonants so many physiological actions modifying the sound in its continuity, or momentarily stopping it altogether.

Vocal sound may be conveniently imagined to proceed as in a sequence of cones of sound arranged base to base and apex to apex—the Broad Vowels forming the base and the Narrow Vowels the apex of each cone. The fundamental principle underlying this fact is that which underlies every action in nature—namely the need for rest to follow on effort, and effort on rest, if there is to be progression. The rule of '**leathan ri leathan agus caol ri caol**,' however inconvenient it may sometimes appear, is an expression of this natural necessity. Let the organs of voice be set to produce a certain sound as for instance **a** in **fad** *length* or the English word *hat*. If the speech is intended to be continued the organs remain in the **a** position, while the sound is momentarily stopped by **d** or **t**, and when the stop is removed they must emit the sound **a** to which they have remained set during the stop. It is this fact that has expression in the Gaelic rule mentioned, 'Broad (vowel) to broad and narrow to narrow,' hence such forms as **fada, bradan, sodal, cogul,** and **idir, eter,** etc.—the orthography conforms to the physiological conditions. In English it is different. We write *hatter* but no one ever so pronounces it; it is impossible to pronounce it so, and it is always spoken as *hattar*. We must in speaking therefore conform to this rule whether we do or do not think it convenient in writing.

It is this same principle of progression from labour towards rest and from rest to labour which determines the sequence of Consonants also—which has been already briefly referred to. The physiological efforts indicated and expressed by **mbp ngc, ndt** have their resolutions by the reverse processes in coming down again—to rest.

It would not be difficult to show that regard to this essential goes beyond the mere form of words, and that it is the fundamental quality in all true eloquence and good prose writing, as it admittedly is in poetry, but such excursions would be outside the present purpose.

PART II—OF THE PARTS OF SPEECH

THE Parts of Speech in Gaelic may be conveniently divided and arranged as follows: Article, Noun, Adjective, Pronoun, Verb, Adverb, Preposition, Conjunction, and Interjection. Of these the first five are declinable; the other four are indeclinable.

CHAPTER I—OF THE ARTICLE

THE Article is a word placed before a Noun to point it out and to limit its meaning; as, **a' mhuir** *the sea,* **an rìgh** *the king,* **nan òrd** *of the hammers.*

There is only one Article in Gaelic, and it corresponds with the English Definite Article *the*.

The inflections of the Article depend upon the Gender, Number, and Case of the Noun with which it is connected; and its phonetic relation to other words going before it determines certain differences of form.

	SING. MASC.	FEM.	PLUR. MASC. AND FEM.
Nom.	an t-, an (am)	an, an t-	na
Gen.	an, an t-	na	nan (nam)
Dat.	an, an t-	an, an t-	na

The Article has only two or perhaps three primary forms—**an, na,** and **an t-**. **Am** and **nam** are the forms which **an** and **nan** take before labials.

The form **na** remains the same in every position.

The form **an** undergoes certain changes to accord with the initial of a following Noun, or with the termination of a preceding Preposition.

1. If the Noun following has an aspirated initial Consonant **an** drops **n**; as **ceann a' bhrathar** *the head of the brother*, **aig a' charaid** *at the friend*, **labhair e a' bhreug** *he spoke the lie (he told an untruth)*.

2. If a preceding Preposition ends in a Vowel **an** drops **a**, and retains **'n** only, even before initial aspirates; **do 'n phiseig** *to the kitten*, **fo 'n bhord** *under the table*.

3. The form **an t-** is that used before the Nominative of Masculine Nouns beginning with a Vowel; as, **an t-athair** *the father*, **an t-each** *the horse*. Before a Noun with initial s-pure in both genders the Aspirated Cases have **an t-**; thus, **beul an t-sodail** *the mouth of the flattery* (i.e. *a flattering mouth*), **anns an t-suil** *in the eye*, **leis an t-slait** *with the rod*.

If an Adjective beginning with a Vowel comes between the Article and Noun, the Article form is that agreeing with the Noun in Gender and as if it were a Vowel-initial Noun; **an t-aona fear deug** *the eleventh man*, **an aona bean deug** *the eleventh woman*, **an t-ochdamh fear** *the eighth man*, **an t-ard shagart** *the high priest*, **an og-bhean** *the young woman*.

The following statement shows the Article in position before Nouns of both Genders beginning with every letter of the Alphabet, and in such relations with Prepositions as to bring out all the possible forms. It will be instructive to observe the various forms and to study them. The lists will also afford abundant means of exercise to the beginner.

† The article was originally sant. the t- as above is a remnant of the original form. F. See Prof. MacKinnon Celtic Review p 105. Vol II, No 22.

MASCULINE NOUNS
Singular.

NOM.	GEN.	DAT. (aig)	(do)
an t-athair *the father*	an athar	aig an athair	do 'n athair
am bràthair *the brother*	a' bhràthar	a' bhràthair	'n bhràthair
an caraid *the friend*	a' charaid	a' charaid	'n charaid
an duine *the man*	an duine	an duine	'n duine
an t-each *the horse*	an eich	an each	'n each
am fear *the man*	an fhir	an fhear	'n fhear
an gàradh *the garden*	a' ghàraidh	a' ghàradh	'n ghàradh
an t-isean *the gosling*	an isein	an isean	'n isean
an laoch *the hero*	an laoich	an laoch	'n laoch
am mac *the son*	a' mhic	a' mhac	'n mhac
an neul *the cloud*	an neoil	an neul	'n neul
an t-òglach *the youth*	an òglaich	an òglach	'n òglach
am port *the harbour*	a' phuirt	a' phort	'n phort
an righ *the king*	an righ	an righ	'n righ
an sgadan *the herring*	an sgadain	an sgadan	'n sgadan
an sodal *the flattery*	an t-sodail	an t-sodal	'n t-sodal
an tigh *the house*	an tighe	an tigh	'n tigh
an t-uircean *the young pig*	an uircein	an uircean	'n uircean

Plural.

na h-athraichean	nan athraichean	na h-athraichean	na h-athraichean
na braithrean	nam braithrean	na braithribh	na braithribh
na cairdean	nan cairdean	na cairdean	na cairdean

In the Nominative it is **an** before all Consonants except Labials, which have **am**. It is **an t-** before Vowels; and with this exception it is **an** before Vowels and Liquids always—in all Cases of both Genders.

In the aspirated Cases, Genitive and Dative, **an** drops **n** before all aspirated Consonants for a reason already given; but Dentals, to which this reason does not apply, are not aspirated and **n** is retained. **S**-mute cannot take aspiration and **n** is therefore retained. By aspiration **f** becomes entirely quiescent and the Noun therefore is as a Vowel-initial Noun. Initial **s**-pure has **an t-** in these Cases.

FEMININE NOUNS

SINGULAR.

NOM.	GEN.	DAT. (aig)	(do)
an abhainn *the river*	na h-aibhne	aig an abhainn	do 'n abhainn
a' bhreug *the lie*	na breige	a' bhreig	'n bhreig
a' chearc *the hen*	na circe	a' chirc	'n chirc
an duthaich *the country*	na duthcha	an duthaich	'n duthaich
an eala *the swan*	na h-eala	an eala	'n eala
an fhìrinn *the truth*	na fìrinne	an fhìrinn	'n fhìrinn
a' ghòraich *the folly*	na gòraiche	a' ghòraich	'n ghòraich
an iteag *the feather*	na h-iteige	an iteig	'n iteig
an lach *the wild duck*	na lacha	an lach	'n lach
a' mhathair *the mother*	na mathar	a' mhathair	'n mhathair
an nighean *the daughter*	na h-inghne	an nighinn	'n nighinn
an òrdag *the thumb*	na h-òrdaige	an òrdaig	'n òrdaig
a' phiseag *the kitten*	na piseige	a' phiseig	'n phiseig
an roineag *the hair*	na roineige	an roineig	'n roineig
an sguab *the sheaf*	na sguaibe	an sguaib	'n sguaib
an t-suil *the eye*	na sula	an t-suil	'n t-suil
an tunnag *the duck*	na tunnaige	an tunnaig	'n tunnaig
an uaigh *the grave*	na h-uaighe	an uaigh	'n uaigh

PLURAL.

na h-aibhnichean	nan aibhnichean	na h-aibhnichean	na h-aibhnichean
na breugan	nam breug	na breugan	na breugan
na cearcan	nan cearc	na cearcan	na cearcan

An is the primary form before the Nominative and Dative, but before aspirated initials—Labials and Gutturals—**n** is dropped.

Na is the form for the Genitive Singular and for the Nominative and Dative Plural of both Genders. It takes **h** before Vowels.

Nan is the form for the Genitive Plural of both Genders and it changes to **nam** before Labials.

Observations on the Article

The Primitive Keltic Article was inflected as follows:—

SING. NOM.	GEN.	DAT.	ACC.	PLUR. NOM.	GEN.	DAT.	ACC.
M. send-os	-í	-û	-on	-í	-an	-obis	-ös
F. send-a	-âs	-i	-in	-âs	-ân	-abis	-âs
N. sen	send-i	-û	sen	-â	-an	-obis	-â

The form **an t-** occurs in two distinct positions, as has been shown. That in the Nom. Masc. before Vowels was from the fact that **s** of the termination of the Article became in this position vowel-flanked. Vowel-flanked **s** always got aspirated, and this determined a hardening of the preceding Consonant **d** to **t**. This influence of aspirated **s** may be fully studied in the Third Sing. Fem. of Prepositional Pronouns, p. 140.

The form **an t-** before initial **s** followed by a Vowel or Liquid in the aspirating Cases is somewhat different. It is not as some have thought a necessity arising from the quiescence of **s** by reason of its aspiration. If the quiescence of **s** and the reduction of the Noun to the state of a Vowel-initial Noun were the cause then **f** which also undergoes this change would need the same form. The correct explanation is in that the old form of the Article for the Cases in which this form now appears was **ind**—for primitive Vowel-ending **senda** and **sendi**—which before aspirated **s** hardens to **int** according to rule. The old language was thus

> **ainm indsrotha = ainm an t srutha** *the name of the river.*
> **dondsluagsa = do 'n t-sluaghsa** *to this host.*
> **indserc = an t-seirc** *the charity.*
> **resintsamfuin = roimh an t-Samhuin** *before Halloween.*

As this hardening only occurs before aspirated **s**, and as the aspiration of **s** is not now indicated but by the presence of **t** before it, there is some reason for looking upon **t** as taking the place of the Aspiration, and so an excuse if not even a justification for writing the **t** in association with **s** rather than with the **an** of the Article. The form **an't** is without any excuse; and so also is the form **an-t**, for if there is any reason for separating **t** from **an** it is that it may be attached to the initial **s**.

The causes which have determined the present forms of the Article and the changes on the initial of the Noun are, some of them extremely remote others not so remote, but all of them are based on the abiding disposition towards physiological convenience. The forms and uses of **an t-**, which have been said to be two different things are only different in that they appear to have resulted from the operation of similar factors at different periods of time. The **an t-** before Feminine **s**-pure which has resulted from the hardening of **ind** the old Feminine form, seems to have occurred at a time much later than that to which must be referred the similar hardening of **d** in the stem of the Primitive Article by the same retrogressive influence of aspirated **s**. In old Gaelic it is **indsuil** hardened to **intsuil** now **an t-suil**; and this is the same thing as happened, long before, in the Nominative Masculine of Vowel-initial Nouns, *e.g.* **sendosatir** *the father* in which the Vowel-flanked **s** of the termination of the Article determined the hardening of the **d** in the stem which yet remains as **t**. Feminine **s**-pure Nouns came to the present form thus, **sendasulis** *the eye* had **d** hardened by the aspirated **s** of the initial of the Noun. There is this difference therefore between the two forms of **an t-**, that the **t** of the one is developed within the Article itself, while that of the other owes its existence to initial **s** of the Noun. A study of the Primitive Article, given above, will show that the aspirated Cases are so because the Article in these Cases originally ended in a vowel, and will show also good reason for taking the **h** which appears '*in hiatu*' in the Gen. Sing. and Nom. Plur. Fem. to be derived from aspirated **s** of the termination of the Article.

Briefly, it may be stated that in the Singular **An** is the form for the Genitive and Dative Masculine and for the Nominative and Dative Feminine, and that in these four positions it undergoes the same changes and for the same reasons.

The Nominative Masculine has three forms **An t-**, **An**, **Am** used with an exact regard to euphony.

The Genitive Feminine is always **Na**.

The Plural is alike for both Genders.

It is interesting to observe that the Genitive of **nighean** has not the initial **n**. This is because **n** does not rightly belong to the word. It used to be **ind ingen**, *the daughter*, and the **n** is that of the Article become attached. The same thing has happened to **an ti** *the person*, which is for **ant i**, and to the word **deigh** *ice*, which used to be **eigh**. The English *nickname=an eke name* and *newt=an ewt* show the same process, and names and place-names show it freely.

CHAPTER II—OF NOUNS

A NOUN is the name of any Person, Object, or Thing whatsoever that we have occasion to mention.

Nouns are classed as Common, Proper, Abstract, and Collective.

A Noun is said to be Common when it is a name common to a class, Proper when it is limited to one person, place, or special object, Abstract when it is the name of the mental conception of a quality or action or state of any object, and Collective when a number of persons or things are viewed as one whole; as, **duine** *a man*, **Duneidin** *Edinburgh*, **naire** *shame*, **leisg** *sloth*, **an t-arm** *the army*, **a' chuideachd** *the company*.

In treating of this Part of Speech we have to consider the GENDER and the DECLENSION of Nouns.

OF GENDER.—In imposing names on sensible objects the great and obvious distinction of sex in the animal world suggested the expediency of inventing names not only for the particular species of animals but also for distinguishing their sex; such are, *vir*, *femina*; bull, cow; **coileach, cearc.**

To mark at once identity of species and diversity of sex the same word with a slight change on its form was applied to both sexes; as, *equus, equina*; lion, lioness; **oglach, banoglach.**

In most languages distinction of sex has been marked not only thus by the form of the Noun but further by the form of the Adjective connected with the Noun. Most Adjectives were furnished with two forms the one of which indicated its connection with the name of a male the other its connection with that of a female. The one was called by grammarians the Masculine Gender the other the Feminine Gender of the Adjective. Adjectives possessing thus a twofold form must necessarily have appeared under one or other of these forms with whatever Noun they happened to be conjoined. Even Nouns significant of inanimate objects came thus to possess one mark of Nouns discriminative of sex according as they happened to be accompanied by an Adjective of the Masculine or of the Feminine Gender. If any Noun was observed to be usually coupled with an Adjective of the Masculine Gender it was termed by grammarians a Masculine Noun, if it was found usually coupled with an Adjective of the Feminine Gender it was termed a Feminine Noun. Thus a distinction of

Nouns into Masculine and Feminine came to be noted and this also was called Gender.

It is observable then that Gender in grammar is taken in two different acceptations. When applied to an Adjective it signifies a certain *form* by which *bonus* is distinguished from *bona*. When applied to a Noun it signifies a certain relation of the word to the attributives connected with it, by which *amor* is distinguished from *cupido*. As sex is a natural characteristic pertaining to living objects, so Gender is a grammatical characteristic pertaining to Nouns—the names of objects whether animate or inanimate.

The Gender of Nouns is not properly speaking indicated; it is constituted by that of the attributives conjoined with them. If there were no distinction of Gender in Adjectives, Participles, etc., there could be none in Nouns. When we say that *amor* is a Noun of the Masculine Gender and *cupido* a Noun of the Feminine Gender, we do not mean to intimate any distinction between the things signified by these Nouns; we mean nothing more than to state a *grammatical* fact, namely, that an Adjective connected with *amor* is always of the same form as when joined to a Noun denoting a male, and that an Adjective connected with *cupido* is always of the same form as when joined to a Noun denoting a female.

When an Adjective was to be connected with a Noun that denoted an object devoid of sex, it is not always easy to guess what views might have determined the speaker to use the Adjective in one Gender rather than in the other. Perhaps sex was attributed to the object signified by the Noun. Perhaps its properties were conceived to bear some resemblance to the qualities characteristic of sex in living creatures. In many instances the form of the Noun seems to have decided the point. But it must be confessed that in this mental process the judgment has been often swayed by trivial circumstances and guided by fanciful analogies. At least it cannot be denied that in Gaelic, where all Nouns are classed either as Masculine or Feminine, the Gender has been fixed by a procedure whereof the grounds cannot now be fully investigated or ascertained. Neither the natural nor the artificial qualities or uses of things named, nor the forms of the names given them, furnish any invariable rule by which the Gender of Nouns may be known. It ought to be remembered however that Gaelic is far from being singular in this respect. The oldest language with which we are acquainted, as well as some of the most polished modern tongues, stand in the same position.

Note.—I flatter myself that all my readers who are acquainted with any of the ancient or modern languages which have distinction of Gender in their attributives will readily perceive that the import of the term Gender in the grammar of those languages is precisely what I have stated above. The same term has been introduced into the grammar of the English tongue, rather improperly, because in an acceptation different from what it bears in the grammar of all other languages. . . . It seems to be a mis-stated compliment which is usually paid to English when it is said that 'this is the only language which has adapted the Gender of its Noun to the constitution of Nature.' The fact is that it has adapted the *Form* of some of the most common names of living creatures and a few of its pronouns to the obvious distinction of *male* and *female* and *inanimate*, while it has left its Nouns without any mark characteristic of Gender. The same thing must happen to any language which abolishes the distinction of Masculine and Feminine in its attributives. If all languages had been constructed on this plan, it may be confidently affirmed that the grammatical term Gender would never have come into use. The compliment intended and due to English might have been more correctly expressed by saying that 'it is the only language that has rejected the unphilosophical distinction of Gender by making its attributives in this respect indeclinable.'—STEWART.

The following observations will go a good way to assist in the determination of the Gender of Nouns.

OF LIVING CREATURES.—The names of males are Masculine, and the names of females are Feminine.

Except (1) **Sgalag** *a farm-servant*, which though it always signifies a male servant yet takes the grammatical declension and relations of a Feminine Noun, *e.g.* **lamh na sgalaige moire** *the hand of the big farm-servant*, in which several points indicate the Feminine Gender. The Article is the Genitive Feminine form, the word **sgalaige** is a Genitive Feminine form and the Adjective has the inflection of the Genitive Feminine in agreement with it, and the Adjective is not aspirated as it would be if the Noun were Masculine.

(2) **Boirionnach** *a woman*, **mart** *a cow*, **capull** *a mare*, which though Feminine in signification, are of the Masculine Gender—the reverse exactly of **sgalag**, and the same explanation applies; **ceann a' bhoirionnaich choir** *the head of the kind woman*, **air muin a' chapuill bhàin** *on the back of the white mare*, **am mart donn** *the dun cow*, not as **a' bhó dhonn** *the dun cow*, which is Feminine in Gender as in sex.

Many Nouns signifying the young of animals are Masculine, regardless of sex; **uan** *a lamb*, **isean** *a gosling*, **laogh** *a calf*.

Nouns denoting a species may be of either Gender; as, **leòmhan** *a lion*, **cat** *a cat*, **asal** *an ass*, **caora** *a sheep*. There is a tendency, determined by some leading characteristic, to make an animal species of one Gender rather than the other. Thus a lion is in conception always Masculine because of its strength, while an ass or a sheep is Feminine for perhaps the opposite reason.

The sex is made specific for such Nouns by adding the Adjectives **firionn** *male* and **boirionn** *female*; as, **cat-firionn** *a male cat*, **laogh-boirionn** *a she-calf*. In the case of wild animals the simple Noun is usually Feminine and the Masculine is made by prefixing the word **boc** *a buck*; **boc-earba** *a roebuck*, **boc-goibhre** *a he-goat*.

OF INANIMATE OBJECTS.—The names of trees and timbers are Masculine; as **darach** *oak*, **giubhas** *fir*, **uinnsean** *ash*: but collective names of trees are Feminine; as, **giubhsach** *a fir-wood*, **iubhrach** *a yew-copse*, **droighneach** *a thorny brake*.

Names of countries are usually Feminine; **Albain** *Scotland*, **Eirinn** *Ireland*. So also are the names of heavenly bodies, musical instruments, and diseases; **grian** *sun*, **gealach** *moon*, **clàrsach** *a harp*, **piob** *a pipe*, **teasach** *a fever*, **a' bhreac** *the smallpox*.

For the rest, the Gender of the names of inanimate objects is determined by the form of the Noun more than by any other accident or circumstance, and the most comprehensive expression of principle on this basis would seem to be that *Nouns in which the final or characteristic Vowel is Broad are Masculine and Nouns in which it is Small are Feminine*; as, **balla** *a wall*, **bàs** *death*, **bròn** *sorrow*, **sùgh** *sap*, which are Masculine, and **deile** *a plank*, **cìr** *a comb*, **clais** *a furrow*, which are Feminine.

There are many exceptions to this statement, but there can be no doubt that the principle underlies the Gender of Nouns in a very interesting degree. In the First Declension Nouns with final **a** are with few exceptions Masculine, and those with final **e** are in somewhat the same proportion Feminine. All that large class of Abstract Nouns in **e** formed from Adjectives are without exception Feminine. In the Third Declension the only exceptions are a few monosyllables, p. 48. In the Second Declension all Feminine Nouns are exceptions; still it is not difficult to see that the principle operates here also.

The only important general exceptions to the principle are Diminutives in **ag**, Abstract Nouns in **achd**, and those Abstract Nouns in **ad** forming the so-called Third Comparative of Adjectives, which though ending in a Broad Vowel are of the Feminine Gender; and Nouns ending in **air, eir, ire, iche** denoting the Agent, which are Masculine.

Summary Statement.

MASC.	FEM.
Names of Males — except **sgalag**.	Names of Females—except **mart, capull, boirionnach**.
Names of Trees singly.	Names of Trees collectively.
Names of Young of Animals.	Names of Countries, Diseases, Musical Instruments, Heavenly bodies.
Names of which last Vowel is Broad—except **ag, achd, ad**.	Names of which last Vowel is Small—except **air, eir, ire, iche**, Agent.

c

There is a small margin of Nouns for which the Gender is not fixed, being Masculine in one place and Feminine in another.

Some Personal Nouns form the Feminine by prefixing **ban** *woman* or *wife* to the Masculine; as **òglach** *a young man-servant,* **ban-oglach** *a maid-servant.* The initial Consonant of the Masculine is aspirated where that is possible, and then **ban** becomes **bana**; as, **bana-mhaighstir** *a mistress*; and where correspondence makes it necessary i is introduced; so, **bain-tighearna** *a lady.*

Cruinne *the globe* and **talamh** *the earth* are Masculine, but their Genitive Case is Feminine; **righ na cruinne** *the king of the globe,* **aghaidh na talmhainn** *the face of the earth.*

The changes expressive of RELATION are made on Nouns in two ways; (1) On the beginning of the Noun (2) On its termination. The relations denoted by changes on the termination are different from those denoted by changes on the beginning, and these changes need not go together —the one may take place without the other. It seems proper therefore to class the changes on the termination by themselves in one division and give it a name, and the changes on the beginning also by themselves in another division and give it a different name—Aspiration. As the changes on the termination denote in general the same relations as are denoted by the Greek and Latin Cases that seems a sufficient reason for adopting the term Case into Gaelic grammar, and applying it as in Greek and Latin to signify 'the changes made on the termination of Nouns or Adjectives to mark relation.' According to this description of them there are Five Cases in Gaelic—Nominative, Genitive, Dative, Accusative, and Vocative.

The Nominative is used when any person or thing is mentioned as the subject of a proposition or question. The Genitive corresponds to an English Noun preceded by *of*. The Dative is only used after some Prepositions. The Accusative is the object of an action or affection. The Vocative is employed when a person or thing is addressed.

Notwithstanding that for Nouns the form of the Accusative is always the same as that of the Nominative, the Case is profitably retained by reason of its logical advantage and its historical continuity. The logical advantage of an Accusative or Objective Case need not be argued; it is so very manifest, even if it were not grammatically justifiable. The historical continuity of the language makes the Accusative absolutely necessary; and there are as many Accusative forms yet remaining as would justify its retention independently of this consideration.

DECLENSION OF NOUNS

Abstract Nouns in **e** of the form of the First Comparative and in **ad** of the form of the Third Comparative so called, as well as Derivatives in **achd**, are indeclinable; as, **géire** *sharpness*, **daoiread** *dearness*, **mórachd** *majesty*.

Nouns that are declinable may be conveniently divided into three Declensions.

FIRST DECLENSION

The First Declension embraces Nouns ending in a Vowel, and all such Nouns as, having a Broad Vowel characteristic, are not declined in the Singular.

Nouns which form the Genitive in **a** though inconsistent with the definition are also put under this Declension for the following reasons :—

1. Because they are like the other Nouns of the Declension in structure and grammatical relations—in all but the form of the Genitive.

2. Because they are a small and diminishing class in a state of transition, tending to drop the **a** of the Genitive and so to fall into the regular Declension.

3. It is not always easy to be sure when this form of the Genitive should be retained in such words, for instance, as **guth** *a voice*, **dath** *colour*, **sruth** *a current*, **ceum** *a step*, and several others.

4. It is not certain whether such words as **calp** *the calf of the leg*, **dealt** *dew*, **earb** *a roe*, **sneachd** *snow* which have the Genitive in **a** ought not to have **a** in the Nominative also—in which case they are of the regular Declension.

5. If Nouns which make the Genitive in **a** were put in a Declension by themselves this uncertainty of the Genitive in the one class and of the Nominative in the other would present a difficulty which is avoided by taking them together.

6. Some Nouns of the Regular Declension ending in **a** have a form of the Plural in **nan**; as, **teanga** *the tongue*, **teanga-nan** *tongues*, and Nouns also of the class that makes the Genitive in **a** have this form; as, **beum** *a stroke*—**beum-a-nan** *strokes*, **ceum** —*a step* **ceumanan** *steps*. No other class of Nouns takes this form; so if it does not show an essential kinship it clearly shows an advantage to have these together.

With the exception just referred to, Nouns of this Declension are not declined in the Singular.

The Plural

Almost all Abstract Nouns and many Collective Nouns are not used in the Plural; as, **smachd** *control*, **teas** *heat*, **dream** *a people*.

Nominative.—Nouns of the First Declension form the Nominative Plural by adding **an** to the Nominative Singular; as, **reachd** *a rule*—**reachd-an**, **eas** *a waterfall*—**easan**, **lios** *a garden*—**liosan**; but

1. Nouns which have the Nominative Singular in a can only take **n** of the **an** in the Nominative Plural; as, **teanga** *a tongue*—**teanga-n**, **marsanta** *a merchant*—**marsantan**.

Nouns that make the Genitive Singular in a have sometimes a peculiar double form of the Plural as well as the ordinary form.

	Gen. Sing.	Nom. Plur.
calp *calf of the leg*	**calpa**	**calpan** and **calpanan**
lagh *law*	**lagha**	**laghan** and **laghanan**
ceum *a step*	**ceuma**	**ceuman** and **ceumanan**

2. Nouns of this Declension ending in a vowel take, with few exceptions, what may be for convenience called an Euphonic form of the Plural in which **t**, **th** or **ch** is introduced for phonetic convenience; as, **coille** *a wood*—**coill-t-ean**, **cno** *a nut*—**cno-th-an**, **balla** *a wall*—**balla-ch-an**.

But since this mode of forming the Plural obtains in all three Declensions it will be well to study the formation specially at this point.

The Euphonic Plural

This Plural is formed by the introduction of **th, t** or **ch** before the plural termination as follows:—

Th is only used in the First Declension and for monosyllables ending in a vowel; **cno** *a nut*—**cno-th-an**, **cro** *a fold*—**croithean**.

T is used in the First Declension for a few Nouns in **le** and **ne**, and in the Third for all monosyllables ending in **l** and **n**; **mile** *a thousand*—**mil.t-ean**, **teine** *fire*—**tein.t-ean**; **tuil** *a flood*—**tuiltean**, **smuain** *a thought*—**smuaintean**.

If Nouns like **mile, teine, coille, baile** were written without the terminal **e**, as some perhaps might be, then **t** would be used for Third Declension only.

Ch is used in all three Declensions and always for words of more than one syllable.

(*a*) In Nouns of First Declension ending in a Vowel, **reatha** *a ram*—**reatha-ch-an**, **balla** *a wall*—**ballachan**, **deile** *a plank*—**deile-a-ch-an**, **cridhe** *a heart*—**cridheachan**.

(*b*) In Nouns of Second Declension ending in **al** and **ar**; **ceangal** *a bond*—**ceang.la-i-ch-ean**, **tobar** *a well*—**tob.ra-i-ch-ean**.

(*c*) In Nouns of Third Declension ending in **air** and **ir**; **nathair** *a serpent*—**nath.r-a-i-ch-ean**, **staidhir** *a stair*—**staidh.r-i-ch-ean**.

Righ *a king* takes **r** in the plural—**righrean**; so **gniomh** *a deed*—**gniomharan**.

It will be observed that this introduction of **t, th,** or **ch** causes certain Vowel changes in order to conform with the Vowel Law of Correspondence, as follows:—

1. When a word ends in a Broad Vowel conformity

follows from the addition of **an**; **cno-th-an, balla-ch-an, reatha-ch-an,** but

In many cases where this correspondence of the Vowels running through three syllables would cause a disagreeable monotony of pronunciation, *e.g.* **còta-ch-an, bata-ch-an** a Narrow Vowel is introduced before and after **ch** for the sake of modulation; and therefore it is **còta-i-ch-e-an, bata-i-ch-e-an.** The principle governing the introduction of these Vowels is difficult to express, for sometimes in what would seem to be exactly similar circumstances they are not introduced; as, **gàta-ch-an, bollachan, cannachan.**

2. When a word ends in a Narrow Vowel it may be brought into correspondence by a Broad Vowel before **ch th** or **t** or a Narrow Vowel after it; as, **deile** *a plank*—**deile-a-ch-an, uisge** *water*—**uisgeachan, cridhe** *a heart*—**cridheachan, coille** *a wood*—**coill . t-e-an.**

A few dissyllables of the First and all dissyllables of the Second and Third Declensions which take this Euphonic Plural syncopate the second syllable.

	SINGULAR.	PLURAL.
1st *Declension.*	mile *a thousand*	mil . t-e-an
,,	baile *a town*	bail . tean
2nd *Declension.*	leabhar *a book*	leabh . r-a-i-ch-ean
,,	meadar *a cogue*	mead . raichean
3rd *Declension.*	cathair *a chair*	cath . . raichean
,,	iuchair *a key*	iuch . . raichean
,,	litir *a letter*	lit . r-i-ch-ean
,,	staidhir *a stair*	staidh . richean

It should be remembered that the word Euphonic is here used for convenience only. Nouns like **cnò, coille,** and **nathair** have **t** and **ch** as part of the old stem, but a great many Nouns coming under this head have not such stems.

It will be noticed that a double correspondence occurs in such words as have a Broad Vowel in the first syllable. In **cathraichean**, for instance, the second **a** is introduced to correspond with the **a** of the first syllable. The second correspondence of **i** and **e** has already been explained.

The *Genitive* is like the Nom. Singular; the *Dative* is like the Nominative; and the *Vocative* adds **a** to the Genitive.

EXAMPLES—MASCULINE NOUNS

		an opinion	*a waterfall*	*a nut*	*a sheepfold*	*a jug*
Sing.	Nom.	beachd	eas	cnò	crò	canna
	Gen.	beachd	eas	cnò	crò	canna
	Dat.	beachd	eas	cnò	crò	canna
	Voc.	a bheachd	'eas	a chnò	a chrò	a channa
Plur.	Nom.	beachd-an	eas-an	cno-th-an	crò-i-th-e-an	canna-ch-an
	Gen.	beachd	eas	cno	crò	canna
	Dat.	beachd-an	easan	cnothan	cròithean	cannachan
	Voc.	a bheachd-a	'easa	a chnotha	a chròtha	a channacha

FEMININE NOUNS

Sing.	Nom.	bàta *a boat*	teanga *a tongue*	ceum *a step*
	Gen.	bàta	teanga	ceuma
	Dat.	bàta	teanga	ceum
	Voc.	a bhàta	a theanga	a cheum
Plur.	Nom.	bàta-i-ch-e-an	teanga-n *or* -nan	ceuma-n *or* -nan
	Gen.	bàta	teanga	ceum
	Dat.	bàtaichean	teangan *or* -nan	ceuman *or* -nan
	Voc.	a bhàtacha	a theangana	a cheuma

SECOND DECLENSION

The Second Declension embraces all such Nouns as, having the characteristic Vowel Broad, are declined in the Singular, as, **bàs** *death*, **bròn** *sorrow*, **sùgh** *sap*.

THE SINGULAR

Genitive.—The Genitive is formed by inserting **i** after the characteristic vowel; and the Feminine in addition takes a terminal short **e**.

Masc.		Fem.	
NOM.	GEN.	NOM.	GEN.
bàs	bais *death*	cluas	cluaise *an ear*
bròn	broin *sorrow*	bròg	broige *a shoe*
sùgh	suigh *sap*	cròg	croige *a claw*

Like these—*Masc.* **ròs** *a rose*, **lòn** *a meadow*, **dùn** *a heap*.
    Fem. **tuagh** *a hatchet*, **fròg** *a hole, den*, **màg** *a paw*.

The following variations of the rule are to be observed, namely that after **i** is inserted:—

    1. **a** + **i** becomes **oi**.

Masc.		Fem.	
NOM.	GEN.	NOM.	GEN.
crann	croinn *a tree, mast*	cas	coise *a foot*
dall	doill *a blind person*	clach	cloiche *a stone*
Gall	Goill *a Lowlander*	bas	boise *a palm (of the hand)*

Masc. **gad** *a wythe*, **fàd** *a turf*.
Fem. **fras** *a shower*, **clann** *children*, **bann** *a hinge*.

2. a+i and o+i become ui.

Masc.		Fem.	
Nom.	Gen.	Nom.	Gen.
alt	uilt *a joint*	long	luinge *a ship*
bolg	builg *a bag*	corc	cuirce *a knife*
calg	cuilg *a bristle*	lorg	luirge *a track*

Masc. **torc** *a boar,* **tonn** *a wave,* **carn** *a heap of stones.*

Fem. **tromp** *a trumpet,* **pong** *a point (of a subject).*

3. ea+i and io+i become i.

Masc.		Fem.	
Nom.	Gen.	Nom.	Gen.
breac	bric *a trout*	breac	brice *the smallpox*
fear	fir *a man*	cearc	circe *a hen*
siol	sil *seed*	crioch	criche *an end*

Masc. **ceann** *a head,* **gleann** *a glen,* **fitheach** *a raven.*

Fem. **leac** *a flagstone,* **cioch** *a teat,* **cailleach** *a hag.*

Mac *a son* and **nighean** *a daughter* may be conveniently placed under this variation. **Gleann** has sometimes **glinne** in Gen. Sing. and **t** in Plural—**gleanntan**.

4. ea+i becomes ei.

Masc.		Fem.	
Nom.	Gen.	Nom.	Gen.
each	eich *a horse*	fearg	feirge *wrath*
ceard	ceird *a tinker*	leas	leise *the thigh*

Masc. **cuilean** *a puppy,* **eilean** *an island.*

Fem. **duilleag** *a leaf,* **caileag** *a lass,* **cuigeal** *a distaff.*

5. ia+i becomes ei.

Masc.			Fem.		
NOM.	GEN.		NOM.	GEN.	
fiadh	feidh	*a deer*	grian	greine	*the sun*
iasg	eisg	*a fish*	iall	eille	*a thong*

Masc. **sliabh** *a hillside,* **cliabh** *a basket, the chest,* **ciall** *sense.*

Fem. **sgiath** *a shield,* **cliath** *a harrow, trellis,* **sgian** *a knife,* gen. **sgeine** and **sgine.**

6. eu+i becomes ei.

Masc.			Fem.		
NOM.	GEN.		NOM.	GEN.	
seun	sein	*an amulet*	breug	breige	*a lie*
treun	trein	*a hero*	meus	meise	*a shallow dish*
meud	meid	*magnitude*	geug	geige	*a branch*

7. eu+i becomes eoi.

Masc.			Fem.		
NOM.	GEN.		NOM.	GEN.	
neul	neoil	*a cloud*			
feur	feoir	*grass*			

leus *a torch,* **beul,** *a mouth,* **meur** *a finger.*

8. eo+i becomes iui.

Masc.,			Fem.		
NOM.	GEN.		NOM.	GEN.	
ceol	ciuil	*melody*			
seol	siuil	*a sail*			

Dative.—The Dative Masculine is like the Nominative. The Dative Feminine is like the Genitive without the terminal short **e.**

Vocative.—The Vocative of the Masculine is like the Genitive, that of the Feminine is like the Nominative.

The Plural

Nominative.—The Nominative Plural Masculine is like the Genitive Singular; as, **raimh** *of an oar*—**raimh** *oars.*

The Nominative Plural Feminine adds **an** to the Nominative Singular; as, **sguab** *a sheaf*—**sguaban** *sheaves.*

The Masculine also takes this form in **an**, but monosyllables not by preference; **preas** *a bush*—**preasan** *bushes* but rather **pris, nead** *a nest*—**neadan** but rather **nid**. Nouns of two or more syllables take it by preference; **cladach** *a shore*—**cladaichean, leabhar** *a book*—**leabhraichean.**

Genitive.—The Genitive Plural is like the Nominative Singular for both Masculine and Feminine Nouns; **tarbh** *a bull*—**cinn nan tarbh** *the heads of the bulls*, **geug** *a branch*—**barran nan geug** *the tips of the branches.*

Dative.—The Dative may for both Genders be the same as the Nominative Plural. This form is always correct for Masculine Nouns, only a few taking the form in **aibh** and then only exceptionally. The Feminine, on the other hand, prefers the form in **aibh** except where euphony excludes it as in **baobh** *a fury*, which would be **baobhaibh**, **marbh** *a dead person* **marbhaibh**—forms that are disagreeable.

Vocative.—The Vocative adds **a** to the Genitive; **chas** *of feet* **a chasa** *O feet*, **neul** *of clouds* **a neula** *O ye clouds.*

The **a**-Declension of Stokes, Windisch, and others, which includes Masculine and Feminine Nouns whose stems originally ended in **a**, covers exactly the same ground as this Second Declension; **mac *makva, lòn *lutna, bas *bosta, sròn *srogna.** Mr. Macbain makes Masculine stems end in **o** and he separates Feminine a-stems according to the following scheme which he suggests.

1. WEAK DECLENSION.—Nouns which have no change in the Singular and make the Plural in -**an**, with various modifications.
   a Nouns ending in a Vowel, **cridhe**—Pl. **cridhe-ach-an**.
   b Ending in inclusive Small Vowel, **fàidh *vati-s—faidhean**.
   c Ending in double Mutes, **reachd *rektu—reachd-an**.

2. STRONG DECLENSION.—Nouns with Broad Vowel ending, making the Genitive in **i** and the Plural in **i** inclusive; that is, all Masculine Nouns of the Second Declension; **lòn** Gen. **loin *lutni**; **mac** Gen. **mic *makvi**.

3. MIXED DECLENSION.—Nouns which are Strong in the Singular and Weak in the Plural.
   a Old â-stems, all Feminine, **cearc** Gen. **circe *cercies**.
   b Old i- and u-stems, **suil** Gen. **sula *sulos**, **cath** Gen. **catha *catous**.
   c Old guttural stems, **làir *larex**, Gen. **larach *laracos**.
   d Family names in **air, athair *atir** Gen. **athar *atros**.

4. IRREGULAR NOUNS, **cu *kuo** Gen. **coin *kunos**.

The most important thing to observe is the separation here of Fem. a-stems from the Strong (Second) Declension, and that 1. *b* belongs to the Third Declension. With this difference Mr. Macbain's scheme runs parallel with that given.

EXAMPLES

	Masculine Singular.	Plural.
Nom.	bàs *death*	bàis *deaths*
Gen.	bàis	bàs
Dat.	bàs	bàis
Voc.	a bhàis	a bhàsa

MASCULINE

		1st var.	2nd var.	3rd var.
		a mast	*a joint*	*a trout*
Sing.	*Nom.*	crann	alt	breac
	Gen.	croinn	uilt	bric
	Dat.	crann	alt	breac
	Voc.	a chroinn	'uilt	a bhric
Plur.	*Nom.*	croinn	uilt	bric
	Gen.	crann	alt	breac
	Dat.	croinn	uilt	bric
	Voc.	a chranna	'alta	a bhreaca

FEMININE

		1st var.	2nd var.	3rd var.
		a foot	*a ship*	*a hen*
Sing.	*Nom.*	cas	long	cearc
	Gen.	coise	luinge	circe
	Dat.	cois	luing	circ
	Voc.	a chas	a long	a chearc
Nom.	*Plur.*	casan	longan	cearcan
	Gen.	cas	long	cearc
	Dat.	casaibh	longaibh	cearcaibh
	Voc.	a chasa	a longa	a chearca

EXAMPLES

Feminine Singular.	Plural.
bròg *a shoe*	brògan *shoes*
bròige	bròg
bròig	brògaibh
a bhròg	a bhròga

NOUNS

4th var.	5th var.	6th var.	7th var.	8th var.
a Highlander	*a deer*	*a hero*	*a cloud*	*a sail*
Gaidheal	fiadh	treun	neul	seol
Gaidheil	feidh	trein	neoil	siuil
Gaidheal	fiadh	treun	neul	seol
a Ghaidheil	'fheidh	a threin	a neoil	a shiuil
Gaidheil	feidh	trein	neoil	siuil
Gaidheal	fiadh	treun	neul	seol
Gaidheil	feidh	trein	neoil	siuil
a Ghaidheala	'fhiadha	a threuna	a neula	a sheola

NOUNS

4th var.	5th var.	6th var.
a thigh	*a sun*	*a branch*
leas	grian	geug
leise	greine	geige
leis	grein	geig
a leas	a ghrian	a gheug
leasan	grianan	geugan
leas	grian	geug
leasaibh	grianaibh	geugaibh
a leasa	a ghriana	a gheuga

THIRD DECLENSION

The Third Declension embraces all Nouns that have the characteristic Vowel Small; as, **caraid** *a friend*, **aimsir** *time*, **tigh** *a house*, **ainm** *a name*.

As an **e** characteristic does not occur in modern Gaelic this Declension is in **i** only.

The Singular

Genitive.—The Genitive is like the Nominative, but the Feminine adds a terminal short **e**.

Masc.		Fem.	
NOM.	GEN.	NOM.	GEN.
faidh	faidh *a prophet*	clais	claise *a furrow*
breid	breid *a patch*	cir	cire *a comb*
iasgair	iasgair *a fisher*	cuilc	cuilce *a reed*

Masc. **eunadair** *a fowler*, **deoiridh** *a weakling*, **righ** *a king*.

Fem. **ceist** *a question*, **truaill** *a sheath*, **snaim** *a knot*.

A few Masculine monosyllables take **e** in the Genitive; as,

NOM.	GEN.	NOM.	GEN.
tigh *a house*	tighe	**bid** *a chirp*	bide
im *butter*	ime	**ainm** *a name*	ainme

Though **ubh** *an egg* has a Broad Vowel, it is a Masculine Noun with Genitive in **e**—**ubh** gen. **uibhe**. It is the only Noun of the kind in the language.

A few Nouns syncopate the sound of the second syllable and, where necessary, i is introduced in the first syllable for correspondence :—

NOM.	GEN.	NOM.	GEN.
dìsinn *a die*	dìsne	gobhainn *a smith*	goibhne
oisinn *a corner*	oisne	maduinn *a morning*	maidne
abhainn *a river*	aibhne, abhna, or abhann		

Dìsinn, oisinn and a few others are often spelled as in ean ; dìsean, oisean.

Some take a in the Genitive, and therefore i of the first syllable is dropped.

NOM.	GEN.	NOM.	GEN.
duthaich *a country*	duthcha	buain *a reaping*	buana
gamhuinn *a stirk*	gamhna	flacail *a tooth*	flacla
cnaimh *a bone*	cnamha		

A number of Feminine Nouns of more than one syllable ending in **air, ir, ail** and **eir** make the Genitive in **ach**, and those in **air**, and some in **ir** syncopate the vowel sound of the final syllable ; **cathair** *a chair, a seat*—**cath.r-ach, nathair** *a snake*—**nath.r-ach,** litir *a letter*—**lit.reach, staidhir** *a stair*—**staidh.r-e-ach.**

Nouns in **ail** suppress i of the final syllable; as, **anail** *breath* — **ana.l-ach, barail** *opinion*—**bara.l-ach, dàil** *delay*—**dà.l-ach, sàil** *a heel*—**sà.l-ach.**

Nouns in **eir** and some in **ir** do not syncopate; as, **dinneir** *dinner*—**dinneireach, aimsir** *time*—**aimsire.**

There is a strong tendency to depart from these forms of the Genitive, and to fall into the regular form, **iuchair-e, dinneir-e,** barail-e, anail-e, staidhr-e, litir-e, nathair-e, cathair-e. It is only with Nouns in **air** and **ir** that the Genitive in **ach** is ordinarily used.

Mathair *a mother*, **athair** *a father*, **brathair** *a brother* and **seanair** *a grandfather*, **seanmhair** *a grandmother* form the Genitive by dropping **i**, and **piuthar** *a sister* has **peathar**.

Dative.—The Dative Singular of both Genders is like the Nominative.

Vocative.—The Vocative also is like the Nominative.

The Plural

Nominative.—The Nominative Plural is formed by adding **ean** to the Nominative Singular; as, **breid** *a patch*—**breidean**, **smuid** *smoke*—**smuidean**, **seoladair** *a sailor*—**seoladairean**.

Nouns which make the Genitive in **ach**, especially those in **air** and **ir**, have **ch** in the Plural; and a few in **l** and **n** take **t**. (See Euphonic Plural, p. 38.)

Genitive.—Nouns of one syllable have two forms for the Genitive Plural, one like the Nominative Singular and one like the Nominative Plural.

Words of more than one syllable have the two forms for the Masculine, but only one form for the Feminine —that of the Nominative Plural.

DECLENSION OF NOUNS

NOM. SING.	NOM PLUR.	GEN. PLUR.
faidh m. *a prophet*	**faidhean**	**faidh** or **faidhean**
cìr f. *a comb*	**cìrean**	**cìr** or **cìrean**
seoladair m. *a sailor*	**seoladairean**	**seoladair** or **seoladairean**
but **amhainn** f. *a river*	**aimhnichean**	**aimhnichean** only
nathair f. *a serpent*	**nathraichean**	**nathraichean**

Dative.—The Dative is formed from the Nominative Plural by putting **ibh** for **ean**.

In modern speech the Dative is almost always like the Nominative Plural and even in writing the **ibh** termination is not regularly adhered to.

Vocative.—The Vocative is like the Nominative, or is formed from it by dropping **an** of the termination.

EXAMPLES—MASCULINE NOUNS

Sing.				
	Nom.	**breid** *a patch*	**tigh** *a house*	**righ** *a king*
	Gen.	breid	tighe	righ
	Dat.	breid	tigh	righ
	Voc.	a bhreid	a thigh	a righ
Plur.	Nom.	breidean	tighean	righ-r-ean
	Gen.	breid or breidean	tigh or tighean	righ or righrean
	Dat.	breidibh	tighibh	righribh
	Voc.	a bhreide	a thighe	a righre

FEMININE NOUNS

Sing.				
	Nom.	**cir** *a comb*	**cathair** *a chair*	**barail** *an opinion*
	Gen.	cire	cath.rach	bara.lach
	Dat.	cir	cathair	barail
	Voc.	a chir	a chathair	a bharail
Plur.	Nom.	cirean	cathraichean	barailean
	Gen.	cir or cirean	cathraichean	barailean
	Dat.	ciribh	cathraichean	barailean
	Voc.	a chire	a chathraiche	a bharaile

IRREGULAR NOUNS

Singular

	NOM.	GEN.	DAT.	VOC.
A sheep	caora	caorach	caora	a chaora
Peat	mòine	mòna	mòine	a mhòine
A cow	bó	boin, bà	bó	a bhó
A drink	deoch	dibhe	deoch	a dheoch
A dog	cù	coin	cù	a choin
A stomach	brù	bronn	broinn	a bhru
God or *a god*	Dia	Dé	Dia	a Dhé

IRREGULAR NOUNS

Singular

	NOM.	GEN.	DAT.	VOC.
A people	sluagh	sluaigh	sluagh	a shluaigh
An infant	leanabh	leinibh	leanabh	a leinibh
A mountain	beinn	beinne	beinn	a bheinn
A woman	bean	mna	mnaoi	a bhean

IRREGULAR NOUNS

Singular

	NOM.	GEN.	DAT.	VOC.
A sister	piuthar	peathar	piuthair	a phiuthair
A back	druim	droma	druim	a dhruim
Honey	mil	meala	mil	a mhil
Sea	muir	mara	muir	a mhuir
Blood	fuil	fala	fuil	'fhuil
Flesh	feoil	feola	feoil	'fheoil
A share, a part	cuid	codach	cuid	a chuid
A right	còir	corach	còir	a choir
An eye	sùil	sùl, sùla	suil	a shuil

FIRST DECLENSION

Plural

NOM.	GEN.	DAT.	VOC.
caoirich	caorach	caoirich	a chaoirich
mòintean	mòintean	mòintean	a mhòintean
bà	bó	bà	
deochan	deochan	deochan	a dheocha
coin	con	coin	a chona
bruthan	bronn	bronnaibh	a bhrùtha
diathan	dia	dé	a dhiatha

SECOND DECLENSION

Plural

NOM.	GEN.	DAT.	VOC.
sloigh	slògh	slòigh	a shlogha
leanaban	leanaban	leanaban	a leanaba
beanntan	beann	beanntan	a bheannta
mnathan	ban	mnathaibh	a mhnathan

THIRD DECLENSION

Plural

NOM.	GEN.	DAT.	VOC.
peathraichean	peathraichean	peathraichean	a pheathraiche
dromanan	dromanan	dromanan	a dhromana
codaichean	codaichean	codaichean	a chodaiche
coraichean	coraichean	coraichean	a choraiche
suilean	sùl	suilean	a shula

CHAPTER III—OF THE ADJECTIVE

An Adjective is a word used along with a Noun to express some quality of the thing signified by the Noun; as, **duine maith** *a good man*, **nighean ghasda** *a handsome girl*, **feasgar breagh** *a fine evening*, **oidhche dhorch** *a dark night*.

Adjectives undergo changes which mark their relation to other words. These changes are made like those on Nouns, partly on the beginning and partly on the termination. The change on the beginning is by aspirating an initial consonant. The Numbers and Cases like those of Nouns are distinguished by changes on the termination. The Gender is marked partly by the initial form and partly by the termination.

Adjectives follow the same lines of inflection as Nouns, so it will be convenient to class them under three declensions.

The Adjective when it precedes the Noun undergoes no inflection; but it causes aspiration of the Noun; as, **deagh dhuine** *a good man*, **droch bhean** *a bad woman*, **priomh-mhuinntir** *aborigines*.

Adjectives ending in **idh** have no inflection.

Adjectives of more than one syllable have no inflection in the Plural which is like the Nominative Singular Masculine throughout.

FIRST DECLENSION

The First Declension embraces all Adjectives ending in a vowel and all such as, having a broad vowel characteristic, are not declined in the Singular; as, **sona** *lucky,* **briste** *broken,* **bochd** *poor.*

This form of Definition is retained in order to preserve the similarity with the Noun Declension—although Adjectives ending in a vowel have no inflection.

The Participle Passive is an Adjective and agrees with its Noun in every respect as an Adjective of the First Declension; as, **daimh bhiadhta** *fatted oxen,* **tighean gealaichte** *whitened houses.*

Adjectives of this Declension ending in a consonant when used with a Masculine Noun have all the cases of the Singular alike and all the cases of the Plural end in **a**. Such Adjectives when in agreement with a Feminine Noun, take **a** in the Genitive Singular and all the cases of the Plural end in **a**.

		MASCULINE *a lucky lad*		FEMININE *a lucky girl*
Sing.	Nom.		gille sona		caile shona
	Gen.	(*ceann*)	gille shona	(*ceann*)	caile sona
	Dat.	(*aig*)	gille sona	(*aig*)	caile shona
	Voc.		a ghille shona		a chaile shona
Plur.	Nom.		gillean sona		cailean sona
	Gen.	(*cinn*)	ghillean sona	(*cinn*)	chailean sona
	Dat.	(*aig*)	gillean sona	(*aig*)	cailean sona
	Voc.		a ghillean sona		a chailean sona
		a poor lad		*a poor girl*
Sing.	Nom.		gille bochd		caile bhochd
	Gen.	(*ceann*)	gille bhochd	(*ceann*)	caile bochda
	Dat.	(*aig*)	gille bochd	(*aig*)	caile bhochd
	Voc.		a ghille bhochd		a chaile bhochd
Plur.	Nom.		gillean bochda		cailean bochda
	Gen.	(*cinn*)	ghillean bochda	(*cinn*)	chailean bochda
	Dat.	(*aig*)	gillean bochda	(*aig*)	cailean bochda
	Voc.		a ghillean bochda		a chailean bochda

It will be observed that the Vocative of the Adjective is the same as the Genitive for the Masculine and the same as the Nominative for the Feminine. This rule obtains for Singular and Plural and through all the Declensions.

Masculine Nouns cause aspiration of the initial consonant of the Adjective in the Genitive Singular.

Feminine Nouns cause aspiration of the Nominative and Dative Singular.

The Vocative Singular is always aspirated.

There is no aspiration of the Plural.

SECOND DECLENSION

The Second Declension embraces all Adjectives of which the characteristic vowel is Broad, and which are declined in the Singular; as, **bàn** *pale, fair,* **grod** *rotten,* **dubh** *black.*

The Singular of Adjectives of the Second Declension is exactly like similar Nouns of the Second Declension —the Genitive takes **i**, and the Feminine in addition takes a terminal short **e**, and the Dative Feminine is like the Genitive without the terminal **e**.

The Plural ends in **a** in all the cases.

		Masculine *a pale lad*		Feminine *a pale girl*
Sing.	Nom.	gille bàn		caile bhàn
	Gen. (*ceann*)	gille bhàin	(*ceann*)	caile bàine
	Dat. (*aig*)	gille bàn	(*aig*)	caile bhàin
	Voc.	a ghille bhàin		a chaile bhàn
Plur.	Nom.	gillean bàna		cailean bàna
	Gen. (*cinn*)	ghillean bàna	(*cinn*)	chailean bàna
	Dat. (*aig*)	gillean bàna	(*aig*)	cailean bàna
	Voc.	a ghillean bàna		a chailean bàna

The aspiration is the same as in the First Declension.

Like **bàn** are **cam** *crooked,* **slàn** *healthy,* **glas** *grey,* **mór** *great,* **òg** *young,* **saor** *free or cheap,* **ùr** *new.*

The following are variations. They are, so far, analogous to those of Nouns of the Second Declension. After inserting i

1. a+i becomes oi.

	Masculine			Feminine		
NOM.	GEN.	DAT.	NOM.	GEN.	DAT.	
dall	dhoill	dall	dhall	doille	dhoill	*blind*
glan	ghloin	glan	ghlan	gloine	ghloin	*clean*
gann	ghoinn	gann	ghann	goinne	ghoinn	*scarce*

Like these—**mall** *slow.*

2. o+i becomes ui.

	Masculine			Feminine		
NOM.	GEN.	DAT.	NOM.	GEN.	DAT.	
gorm	ghuirm	gorm	ghorm	guirme	ghuirm	*blue*
lom	luim	lom	lom	luime	luim	*naked*
borb	bhuirb	borb	bhorb	buirbe	bhuirb	*fierce*

Like these—**olc** *bad,* **cróm** *bent,* **tróm** *heavy,* **bog** *soft,* **dónn** *brown,* **moch** *early,* **prónn** *pounded.*

3. ea+i and io+i become i.

	Masculine			Feminine		
NOM.	GEN.	DAT.	NOM.	GEN.	DAT.	
breac	bhric	breac	bhreac	brice	bhric	*spotted*
beag	bhig	beag	bheag	bige	bhig	*small*
crion	chrin	crion	chrion	crine	chrin	*very small*

Like these—**geal** *white,* **boidheach** *pretty,* **mion** *minute,* **maiseach** *beautiful,* **coitchionn** *catholic.*

4. ea+i becomes ei.

	Masculine			Feminine		
NOM.	GEN.	DAT.	NOM.	GEN.	DAT.	
tearc	theirc	tearc	thearc	teirce	theirc	*scarce*
dearg	dheirg	dearg	dhearg	deirge	dheirg	*red*
deas	dheis	deas	dheas	deise	dheis	*ready*

Like these—**searbh** *bitter*, **ceart** *right*, **teann** *tight*.

5. ia+i becomes ei.

	Masculine			Feminine		
NOM.	GEN.	DAT.	NOM.	GEN.	DAT.	
liath	leith	liath	liath	leithe	leith	*hoary*
fial	fheil	fial	fhial	feile	fheil	*generous*

Like these—**cian** *far distant*, **ciar** *grey*.

6. eu+i becomes ei.

	Masculine			Feminine		
NOM.	GEN.	DAT.	NOM.	GEN.	DAT.	
geur	gheir	geur	gheur	geire	gheir	*sharp*
treun	threin	treun	threun	treine	threin	*heroic*

Fliuch *wet*, **tiugh** *thick* become **fliche, tighe** for **fliuiche, tiuighe** in Gen. Sing. Fem., and **fada** *long*, **tana** *thin*, **granda** *ugly* take the declension in i—**faide, taine, grainde**. Some syncopate, as **uasal** *noble*—**uaisle, leathan** *broad*—**leithne**.

THIRD DECLENSION

The Third Declension embraces all Adjectives of which the characteristic vowel is small; as, **binn** *melodious*, **glic** *wise*, **tinn** *sick*.

Adjectives of this Declension when in agreement with a Masculine Noun have all the cases of the

THE ADJECTIVE

Singular alike, but when in agreement with a Feminine Noun the Genitive Singular takes **e**. All the cases of the Plural end in **e**.

Compare this with Adjectives of the First Declension ending in a consonant. It is exactly similar—only e for a.

		MASCULINE *a wise lad*		FEMININE *a wise girl*
Sing. Nom.		**gille glic**		**caile ghlic**
Gen.	(*ceann*)	**gille ghlic**	(*ceann*)	**caile glice**
Dat.	(*gu*)	**gille glic**	(*gu*)	**caile ghlic**
Voc.		**a ghille ghlic**		**a chaile ghlic**
Plur. Nom.		**gillean glice**		**cailean glice**
Gen.	(*cinn*)	**ghillean glice**	(*cinn*)	**chailean glice**
Dat.	(*gu*)	**gillean glice**	(*gu*)	**cailean glice**
Voc.		**a ghillean glice**		**a chailean glice**

The Aspiration is the same here as in the other Declensions.

If an Adjective is in agreement with a Masculine Noun of the Second Declension the Aspiration is different.

		MASC. NOUN OF 2ND DEC. *Lowlander*	ADJ. OF 1ST DEC. *lucky*	ADJ. OF 2ND DEC. *pale*	ADJ. OF 3RD DEC. *wise*
Sing. Nom.		**Gall**	**sona**	**bàn**	**glic**
Gen.	(*ceann*)	**Goill**	**shona**	**bhàin**	**ghlic**
Dat.	(*gu*)	**Gall**	**sona**	**bàn**	**glic**
Voc.		**a Ghoill**	**shona**	**bhàin**	**ghlic**
Plur. Nom.		**Goill**	**shona**	**bhàna**	**ghlice**
Gen.	(*cinn*)	**Ghall**	**sona**	**bàna**	**glice**
Dat.	(*gu*)	**Goill**	**shona**	**bhàna**	**ghlice**
Voc.		**a Ghalla**	**sona**	**bàna**	**glice**

The Genitive Singular is aspirated as it is with other Masculine Nouns in all Declensions of the Adjective—and the *plural is aspirated in the Nominative and Dative*. This Aspiration of the Plural is peculiar to Masculine Nouns of the Second Declension.

THE ASPIRATION OF THE ADJECTIVE may be summed up thus:—All Masculine Nouns aspirate the Genitive Singular of the Adjective, and Masculine Nouns of the Second Declension aspirate the Nominative and Dative Plural also.

Feminine Nouns aspirate the Nominative and Dative Singular but never the Plural.

The Vocative Singular of both Genders is always aspirated.

THE NOUN AND ADJECTIVE WITH THE ARTICLE

When a Noun is used with the Article, the Adjective is aspirated in the same cases as it is aspirated by the Noun alone—*and in the Dative Singular Masculine besides.*

This is the only difference which the combination with the Article causes.

COMPARE

			a great lad	*the great lad*	*the lucky Lowlander*
Sing.	Nom.		gille mór	an gille mór	an Gall sona
	Gen.	(ceann)	gille mhóir	a' ghille mhóir	a' Ghoill shona
	Dat.	(aig)	gille mór	a' ghille mhór	a' Ghall shona
Plur.	Nom.		gillean móra	na gillean móra	na Goill shona
	Gen.	(cinn)	ghillean móra	nan gillean móra	nan Gall sona
	Dat.	(aig)	gillean móra	na gillean móra	na Goill shona

THE ADJECTIVE

The following Compound forms may now be studied:

COMPOUND NOUNS are formed in three ways:—

1. By the combination of two Nouns; **lan-mara** *full tide*, **gille-coise** *a footman*.

2. By that of Noun and Adjective; **sgian-dubh** '*sgean-du*' *black knife*.

3. By an Adjective and Noun; **cruaidh-chàs** *hardship*.

When two Nouns combine to form a Compound Noun the first is declined regularly. The second has the Genitive form always and in all the cases. It may be Singular or Plural. If it is Singular, it takes the Aspiration of an Adjective in agreement with the first Noun—if Plural it takes the Aspirate throughout.

	SINGULAR		
	a full tide	*a henhouse*	*a nut-wood*
Nom.	lan-mara	tigh-chearc	coille-chno
Gen.	lain-mhara	tigh-chearc	coille-chno
Dat.	lan-mara	tigh-chearc	coille-chno
Voc.	a lain-mhara	a thigh-chearc	a choille-chno

Compound Nouns retain the Gender of the principal component; **cis-mhaor** *a tax-gatherer*, is Masculine as **maor** is, though **cìs** is Feminine. Except Nouns compounded with **ban**, which are all Feminine.

When a Noun and Adjective combine to form a Compound Noun both parts are regularly declined as if they stood apart.

	SINGULAR	PLURAL
Nom.	coileach-dubh *a black-cock*	coilich-dhubha *black-cocks*
Gen.	coilich-dhuibh	coileach-dubha
Dat.	coileach-dubh	coilich-dhubha
Voc.	a choilich-dhuibh	a choileacha-dubha

Final **n** and **l** of the first element prevents Aspiration of initial Dental of the second; **aig sgoil-dannsa** *at a dancing-school*, **'s a' sgoil-duibh** *in the school of black-art*, lit. *black-school*.

When an Adjective and Noun combine, the Adjective retains the Nominative form throughout, and the Noun is regularly declined and has the Aspiration throughout.

	SINGULAR	PLURAL
Nom.	**dubh-fhocal** *a dark saying*	**dubh-fhocail** *dark sayings*
Gen.	**dubh-fhocail**	**dubh-fhocal**
Dat.	**dubh-fhocal**	**dubh-fhocail**
Voc.	**a dhubh-fhocail**	**a dhubh-fhocla**

COMPOUND ADJECTIVES are formed in two ways:—

1. By the combination of a Noun and Adjective; **bàr-bhuidhe** *yellow-topped*.

2. By that of two Adjectives; **mìn-bhreac** *fine-spotted*.

In Compound Adjectives both the constituent words undergo regular declension and the second is aspirated throughout.

SINGULAR

Nom.	**tonn-gheal** *white-waved*	**ciuin-gheal** *calm-white*
Gen.	**thuinn-ghil**	**chiuin-ghil**
Dat.	**tonn-gheal**	**ciuin-gheal**

These are Masculine forms. It will be well to practise these Adjectives with Feminine Nouns also, and perhaps write them out in full. **Cuan** *an ocean* (m.) **tonn-gheal**, and **fairge** *a sea* (f.) **thonn-gheal**; **latha** *a day* (m.) **ciuin-gheal**, and **oidhche** *night* (f.) **chiuin-gheal**.

Inflectional **e** of the Genitive of the first constituent of the Compound forms is dropped; as, **tigh-chearc** *of a henhouse*—not **tighe, slait-iasgaich** *of a fishing rod*—not **slaite, ceann circe mìn-bhrice** *the head of a fine-spotted hen*—not **mìne.**

But if **e** belongs to the stem of the first word in the Compound, it is not dropped; as, **fad maide-droma** *the length of the rafter*, **duileach coille-chno** *the foliage of a nut-wood.*

COMPARISON OF ADJECTIVES

There are in Gaelic two forms of Comparison which may be named the First and the Second Comparative.

The First Comparative is like the Genitive Singular Feminine of Adjectives; as, **fada** *long*—**faide** *longer*, **bàn** *pale*—**bàine** *paler*, **tróm** *heavy*—**truime** *heavier*.

When an Adjective suffers contraction in the Genitive Singular Feminine the Comparative forms also are contracted; **dileas** *faithful*—**dilse, dilsid,** and **dilsead** Comparatives.

The Second Comparative is formed from the First by changing final **e** to **id**; **bàine**—**bàinid, truime**—**truimid.** It may be translated *paler by, heavier by.*

Is bàinid i sin *she is paler by* (or *because of*) *that.*

Bu truimid e an eallach *he was heavier by* (or *because of*) *the burden.*

By changing **id** of the Second Comparative to **ead** a

form is derived that has been called the THIRD COMPARATIVE;

	1st comp.	2nd comp.	3rd comp.
daor *dear*	**daoire**	**daoirid**	**daoiread** *dearness*
geal *white*	**gile**	**gilid**	**gilead** *whiteness*
dearg *red*	**deirge**	**deirgid**	**deirgead** *redness*

But as this form is not an Adjective but an Abstract Noun it is here referred to only for the purpose of showing its derivation.

The three forms may take Aspiration but they have no inflection.

Adjectives of more than one syllable do not readily admit of a Second Comparative and therefore not of a Third.

Adjectives of two syllables in **ach, ail, eil** and **or** may take the two Comparatives but as such forms are not agreeable they are rarely used; for instance, **is maisichid i sin** *she is more beautiful because of that*, **air a maisichead** *however beautiful she is*—from **maiseach** *beautiful*.

Adjectives in **idh, ionn, da** and Participles in **te, ta** never take these forms.

The SUPERLATIVE which is but a particular mode of expressing Comparison has not a distinct form. This Superlative Comparison is made between one individual or a chosen number of individuals and all others of that kind or class taken together, or between a part and the whole.

The forms **a's** and **bu** are used before the Comparative to express comparison—with the Verbs **is** and **bu**; and **na's, na bu** are used with **tha** and all other Verbs; **is e a's gile** *he is (the) whiter,* **bu e bu ghile** *he was (the) whiter;* **tha e na's gile** *he is whiter,* **bha e na bu ghile** *he was whiter.* When the Second term of the Comparison is specific and expressed, **na** is put after the Adjective; **is e a's gile na mise** *he is whiter than I,* **bha e na bu ghile na mise** *he was whiter than I.*

When the First term in Comparison is specific, and the second is unlimited or expressly inclusive of the whole of which the First is an unit or a part—that is the Superlative form; **an righ a's airde a tha ann** *the king who is highest of all (that are),* **bha Solamh na bu ghlice na iad uile** *Solomon was wiser than them all* = *the wisest.*

It should be observed that the Verbs **is** and **bu** always take the Personal Pronoun next after them even when the Noun is expressed, **is e Domhnull a's gile** *Donald is (the) whiter,* **bu i a' bhean bu ghlice** *she was the wiser woman.*

The forms used in comparison are not quite free from difficulty. The commonly accepted forms are here given, and in regard to **a's**, though it is a departure from the truer form **is**, it may be as well to accept it as involving the Relative with the Verb. The form with **bu** presents a real difficulty. In one position, when the Adjective has a Consonant initial, the Relative is not expressed, and not implied so far as can be made out, **bu e bu mhiosa** *he was the worse,* but when the Adjective has a Vowel initial the Relative is expressed **bu e a b' airde** *he was the higher.* It is not easy to explain this by any exigency of Syntax. It offers a distinct

E

suggestion that the form **a b'** is the reversed form of **bu**—**bu e ub airde**; and let it be remembered that the same expediency operates in other places, as when **do** *thy* becomes **ad** after the Preposition **ann**, and when the Preposition **do** *to* becomes **adh** before Vowels; **a dol a dh' Inbhernis** *going to Inverness*.

Stewart's suggestion that **nas** is for **ni a is** *thing which is* seems to be borne out by older forms; **niis gile** is met with in old texts. The preference for the Broad Sound of **nas** and **na bu** as against the older **nis** and **nibu** is quite regular.

A few Adjectives are more or less irregular in their comparison—

	1st comp.	2nd comp.	3rd comp.
maith *good*	fearr	feairrd	feobhas
mór *great*	mò	mòid	muthad
olc *bad*	miosa	misd	miosad
teth *hot*	teotha	teothaid	teothad
gearr *short*	giorra	giorraid	giorrad
furasda *easy*	fasa	fasaid	fasad
toigh *dear, loved*	tocha		
ionmhuinn *beloved*	annsa		

Other Adjectives usually classed as irregular, **beag** *small*, **cumhang** *narrow*, **duilich** *difficult*, **fagus** *near*, **géur** *sharp*, **laidir** *strong* and **leathan** *broad*, are either quite regular or irregular only by the contraction of the First Comparative.

	1st comp.	2nd comp.	3rd comp.
beag *small*	bige	bigid	bigead
cumhang *narrow*	cuinge (*contr.*)	cuingid	cuingead

Some Adjectives, however, though their own essential forms are quite regular, have other exceptional and perhaps troublesome but extremely interesting forms for the Comparative.

Maith has two forms of the Comparative not etymologically related to itself nor to one another—**fearr** which is used in the First and Second Comparatives but not in the Third, and **feobha** used in the three Comparatives so supplying the defect of **fearr**.

Duilich has Comparative **dorra** which goes regularly into the Second and Third; and similarly, **laidir** has **treasa** and **beag** has **lugha**.

	1st comp.	2nd comp.	3rd comp.
maith	{ fearr { feobha	feairrd feobhaid	——— feobhas
beag	{ bige { lugha	bigid lughaid	bigead lughad
duilich	{ duilghe { dorra	duilghid dorraid	duilghead dorrad
laidir	{ laidire { treasa	laidirid treasaid	laidiread treasad

CHAPTER IV—OF NUMERALS

NUMERAL Adjectives are either Cardinal or Ordinal.

Those classed as CARDINAL are the simple Adjectives of Number; as, **aon duine** *one man*, **tri daoine** *three men*.

The following, which are usually given as Cardinal Numeral Adjectives, are in reality Nouns. They may stand alone as the Subject or Object of a Transitive Verb, and they may be governed by a Preposition—just as a

Noun; **chunnaic a dha mi** *two saw me*, **chunnaic mi a dha** *I saw two*, **sguir e aig a ceithir** *he stopped at four*.

A Noun is of course always understood but it cannot be expressed with these forms. If it were expressed, it should be as **chunnaic da dhuine mi** *two men saw me*, **sguir e aig ceithir uairean** *he stopped at four hours = o'clock*.

These forms come into the proper Numeral Adjective after *forty* and they are therefore given first.

a h-aon *one*	**a sia** *six*	**a h-aon deug** *eleven*
a dha *two*	**a seachd** *seven*	**a dha dheug** *twelve*
a tri *three*	**a h-ochd** *eight*	**a tri deug** *thirteen*
a ceithir *four*	**a naoi** *nine*	**a ceithir deug** *fourteen*
a coig *five*	**a deich** *ten*	and so to **fichead** *twenty*

after which it is **a h-aon ar fhichead** *twenty-one*, **a dha ar fhichead**, etc.

It will be well to show Numeral Adjectives with Nouns thus :—

Cardinal Numerals

aon f hear *one man*	**aon** bhean *one woman*
da f hear *two men*	**da** mhnaoi *two women*
tri fir *three men*	**tri** mnathan *three women*

The Agreement between the Adjective and Noun is the same from and including *three* to *ten*; **ceithir fir** *four men*, **ceithir mnathan** *four women*, and so for **coig** *five*, **sia** *six*, **seachd** *seven*, **ochd** *eight*, **naoi** *nine*, **deich** *ten*.

aon f hear **deug** *eleven men*	**aon** bhean **deug** *eleven women*
da f hear **dheug**	**da** mhnaoi **dheug**
tri fir **dheug**	**tri** mnathan **deug**

And so on like **tri deug** up to

fichead fear *twenty men*	**fichead** bean *twenty women*
aon fhear **ar fhichead**	**aon** bhean **ar fhichead**
da fhear **ar fhichead**	**da** mhnaoi **ar fhichead**
tri fir **ar fhichead**	**tri** mnathan **ar fhichead**

And so like **tri ar fhichead** up to

da fhichead fear *forty men*	**da fhichead** bean *forty women*
da fhichead fear's **a h-aon**	**da fhichead** bean's **a h-aon**
da fhichead fear's **a dha**	**da fhichead** bean's **a dha**

And so on to

ceud fear *a hundred men* **ceud** bean *a hundred women*

And so

da cheud, tri cheud *two hundred, three hundred*, etc., and **mile** *a thousand*.

Aon aspirates all initial Consonants except Dentals **n, d, t, s**.

Da aspirates all initial aspirable Consonants and governs the Dative—or rather a form similar to the Dative.

Though it is customary to say that **da** governs the Dative and that in some positions it is followed by the Genitive, as **buinn mo dha bhroige** *the soles of my two shoes*, the statement is not correct. This Dative so called is really the Accusative of the old Dual Number in such an expression as **chunnaic mi da chloich** *I saw two stones*; and **da**, properly speaking, has no governing influence. The Nominative Dual Feminine was, and is, like the Dative Singular, and the Genitive Dual was like the Genitive Singular. This is the explanation of a peculiarly strange 'exception.'

Deug is an Adjective agreeing with its Noun always; as, **aon fhear deug** *eleven men*, **aon bhròg dheug** *eleven shoes*.

Fichead, ceud, and **mile** take a Noun in the Singular; **fichead fear, ceud bròg, mile fear**.

Ceud is aspirated by **aon, da, tri, ceithir**; as, **aon cheud** *one hundred*, **da cheud, tri cheud, ceithir cheud fear** *four hundred men*. **Ceud** is an old Neuter Noun.

Ar is the aspirating Preposition, p. 122.

Ordinal Numerals

a' cheud fhear *the first man*
an dara fear
an treas fear
an ceathramh fear
an coigeamh fear
an siathamh fear
an seachdamh fear
an t-ochdamh fear
an naoidheamh fear
an deicheamh fear
an t-aona fear **deug**
an dara fear **deug**

a' cheud bhean *the first woman*
an dara bean
an treas bean
an ceathramh bean
an coigeamh bean
an t-siathamh bean
an t-seachdamh bean
an ochdamh bean
an naoidheamh bean
an deicheamh bean
an aona bean **dheug**
an dara bean **dheug**

And so on to

am ficheadamh fear *the 20th man*
an t-aona fear **ar fhichead**
an dara fear **ar fhichead**

an fhicheadamh bean *the 20th woman*
an aona bean **ar fhichead**
an dara bean **ar fhichead**

And so on to

an da fhicheadamh fear *the 40th man*
an da fhicheadamh fear 's a h-aon
an da fhicheadamh fear 's a dha

an da fhicheadamh bean *the 40th woman*
an da fhicheadamh bean 's a h-aon
an da fhicheadamh bean 's a dha

And so on

an tri ficheadamh fear *the 60th man*
an ceudamh fear *the 100th man*

an tri ficheadamh bean *the 60th woman*
an ceudamh bean *the 100th woman*

A **cheud** *the first* is the only Ordinal that causes Aspiration. The form of the Article follows the rules already explained (p. 22). Though the Dental sequence would determine **deug** instead of **dheug** after **bean** the aspirated form is shown here as it is in all aspirable Feminine Nouns ; **an aona bhròg dheug** *the eleventh shoe,* **an aona chaora dheug ar fhichead** *the thirty-first sheep.*

The use of **an t-aon** for *each* or *every one* is interesting ; **tha mac an t-aon aca,** *they have each a son* ; **tha fear an t-aon againn** *we have one* (Masc.) *each* ; **tha té an t-aon againn,** *we have one* (Fem.) *each.*

The form **sia** *six* is perhaps not the truest form etymologically. It is used here because it is more in accord with the modern pronunciation than **sèa** or **sè**.

Ar is more commonly spoken as **air**, and it is often made **thar** which is perhaps an error. That **thar**, even if not so intended, is taken for the Preposition **thar** *across* or *beyond*, there can be no doubt, for it is used in the same way as **thairis** ; **an treas Salm thar an fhichead,** *the twenty-third psalm*=lit. *the third psalm beyond the twenty* ; **an ceathramh Salm thairis air an dà fhichead,** *the forty-fourth psalm*=*the fourth psalm over the two twenties.*

Twenty-one is most commonly **fear ar fhichead, bean ar fhichead** ; and when the units and twenties in a number are the same, 42, 63, 84, it is **da 'us da fhichead,** *two and two twenties,* **tri 'us tri fichead, ceithir 'us ceithir fichead.** **Leth-cheud** *half a hundred* is a favourite expression for *fifty* ; **leth-cheud fear** *fifty men.*

It should be observed that **ceud** *a hundred* being a Noun may take the Article; **ceud fear** *a hundred men,* **an ceud fear** *the hundred men* ; and it is instructive to compare this with **a' cheud fhear** *the first man* in which **ceud** is a simple Adjective agreeing with its Noun quite regularly. **Fear** in **an ceud fear** undergoes no inflection and is not aspirated. **Ceud gu leth** is *a hundred with* (old **Con**) *half.* So other expressions also; **slat gu leth** *a yard and a half*, **mile gu leth**, *a thousand and a half* 1500, or *a mile and a half*.

An dara is interesting as not belonging etymologically to the Numerals. It has its most correct usage in such expression as **an darna cuid**, or **an dala cuid**, not *the second part*, but the *other* or *alternative part*. It is derived from a combination of the old Article with the Adjective **araile**, and later **aile** now **eile**, **indaraile**, or **indaile**, *the other*.

The Ordinals 21st to 30th inclusive are often rendered **an t-aona fear fichead, an dara fear fichead,** etc.

The following are called NUMERAL NOUNS. They have no inflection, and are only applied to persons :—

aonar	*one person*		'**am aonar** *alone*
dithis	*two persons*		old form **días**
triuir	*three*	„	or *three men*, old form
ceathrar	*four*	„	**triar**
cóignear	*five*	„	
sianar	*six*	„	
seachdnar	*seven*	„	
ochdnar	*eight*	„	
naoinear	*nine*	„	
deichnear	*ten*	„	

These Nouns except **aonar** usually take the Genitive Plural of **fear** *a man* or **bean** *a woman* after them, and they are used when a group of so many is spoken of, as against so many individuals. **Triuir fhear** (*a* *group of)* *three men* rather than **tri fir, deichnear bhan** *a group of ten women* rather than **deich mnathan** *ten women.*

CHAPTER V—OF PRONOUNS

THE Pronouns are for the most part words used instead of Nouns. They may be arranged in the following divisions: Personal, Possessive, Relative, Demonstrative, Interrogative.

THE PERSONAL PRONOUNS are of the First, Second, and Third person,—Singular and Plural; and they have a Simple and an Emphatic form.

	SINGULAR.			PLURAL.		
	1	2	3	1	2	3
Simple	**mi** *I*	**tu** *thou*	{ **e** *he* **i** *she* }	**sinn** *we*	**sibh** *you*	**iad** *they*
Emphatic	**mise**	**tusa**	{ **esan** **ise** }	**sinne**	**sibhse**	**iadsan**

There is no distinction in form between the Nominative and Accusative of the First Personal Pronoun, so it may be translated as *I* and *me*. The Nominative of the Second Person may be plain or aspirated, but the Accusative form is always **thu** never **tu**. In the Third Person Masculine and Feminine the forms **e** and **i** are used as a rule for both cases, but **se**, **si** have been used for the Nominative in order to mark a distinction—and this is certainly a grammatical advantage. The forms **se, si,** and **siad** *they* are never used in the Accusative.

Both the Simple and the Emphatic forms of the First and Second Persons may be aspirated but this does not alter their meaning. The **thu** just referred to is the essential Accusative form, always used as the Object to Transitive Verbs, and is not merely determined by necessity of Aspiration; as, **chronaich e thu** *he reproved thee,* **bhuail iad thu** *they struck thee,* but **buailidh tu e** *thou wilt strike him.*

There is a tendency which is grammatically wrong but phonetically almost excusable, to use the unaspirated form after verbals ending in **s**; as, **'s e chrunas tu,** which is meant for *it is he who will crown thee,* but it means the exact opposite, *it is he whom thou wilt crown.* The reason for this tendency is in the fact that **s** always tends to rest in **t** as may be abundantly observed not only in Gaelic but in other languages also. Mr. MacFarlane has shown clearly that 'if the physiological processes for the production of **s** be carried out in detail but substituting complete for partial contact the effect produced is **t**.' So there is almost an excuse for the error here shown; **tu** is used where **thu** should be, because it comes more readily to the organs of voice. This is very interesting as perhaps the only instance in the language of a grammatical form not coinciding with phonetic expediency. When however it is understood that **tu** in such relations is wrong and that **thu** is right, the small difference of phonetic convenience between the one and the other can be no sufficient excuse for indulging the error, but it will always be a good reason that we should guard against an error that comes so readily.

Fein *self,* in the Plural *selves,* may be joined to the Simple forms of the Personal Pronouns in order to convey a greater degree of emphasis than is expressed by the Emphatic form. **Mise** means the same as an emphasised *I* in English; as, **chunnaic mise** *I saw*—whether others saw or not. **Mi-fein** means *I myself*; as, **chunnaic mi-fein e** *I myself saw him*—so I cannot doubt it.

The Pronoun **sibh** *you* of the Plural Number is used almost universally in addressing a single person of superior rank or greater age while **tu** *thou* of the Singular Number is used in addressing an inferior or an equal. The Supreme Being is always addressed by the Pronoun **tu** of the Singular Number.

This is Dr. Stewart's observation, but it is almost certain that age alone and not rank is the determining factor in this usage. It is offensive to the pure spirit of the language to use the Plural form for a young person whatever his rank may be.

THE EMPHATIC FORMS.—However mutilated, deformed, and changed the Pronoun itself is and the added syllable, there can be no doubt that in the Emphatic forms indications of a repetition of the Pronoun may still be observed. A repetition of words is the most elemental method of expressing emphasis in every language, and it causes no surprise if we discover that a repetition of the Pronoun constitutes the Emphatic form in Gaelic. Our pronominal elements are so greatly altered that it is very difficult to see where the kinship of the repeated part is with the other—that is, of the added syllable with the Pronoun proper. In **sibh-se or si-se**, as it is more correctly pronounced, the repetition is comparatively evident. In **sinn-ne** and in **(s)i-se** *she* it is not very obscure. In **(s)e-san** and **(s)iad-san** it is not so clear; and in **mi-se** and **tu-sa** it is difficult to see.

The Welsh language was at one time, very long ago, closely related to Gaelic. We can even imagine a time when the two were identical. In their essential structure and in their old lines and forms we expect to find evidence of the old kinship, and if we could arrive at their primal elements we should expect to find them very much alike, perhaps identical. It is certain that the further we go back in the history of the two languages the more evident does the early kinship become. In this way most valuable light is thrown on the one language by the other, without which this interesting point could not be made so clear.

The Personal Pronouns in Welsh

	SINGULAR			PLURAL		
	1	2	3	1	2	3
Simple	**mi** *I*	**ti** *thou*	**ev** *he* / **hi** *she*	**ni** *we*	**çwi** *you*	**hwynt** *they*
Emphatic	**myvi**	**tydi**	**eve(v)** *m.* / **hyhi** *f.*	**nyni**	**çyçwi**	**hwyntwy(nt)**

It may be explained that **i** sounds *ee* as in Gaelic, that **ç** is like the aspirated **c** of Gaelic in **chi** *will see*, that **y** is like the short *y* in *sundry*, and that **v** is like **mh** of Gaelic.

It will be clearly seen that in every instance the doubling of the Simple Pronoun to form the Emphatic is manifest, though in 3rd Singular **v** of the repeated masculine and **nt** of the 3rd Plural are now lost.

The older Gaelic forms point in the same direction as the following examples from Zeuss show:—

Sing. 1. **is messe rophroidich doib** *it was I who preached to you.*
  nifil and acht meisse moínur *there is not (here) but I alone.*

  2. **nitussu thoénur** *not thou alone.*
  amal tussu *like you.*

  3. **ishese sis andechor** *this is their difference.*
  bá hesse, ba hesseom *it was he.*

Plur. 1. **snisni ata sonorṭu** *it is we who are very strong.*
   isnini firionaib *we are the righteous (persons).*
2. **apstil itossug sissi iarum** *apostles first you afterwards.*
   ississi intempulsin *ye are that temple.*
3. **atcessa iatsom fon cruth sin** *they were seen in that form.*

It will be observed that the First Person Singular and the Third Plural are the only positions in which the repetition is not clearly suggested, and even for these we prefer to await further knowledge before concluding that they have not been formed in the same way—by repetition.

The Emphatic augment may be taken by the Possessive Pronouns, by the Prepositional Pronouns, by Nouns, and by forms of the Verb which have the Nominative inclusive **buaileam, buaileam-sa** *let me strike.*

THE POSSESSIVE PRONOUNS correspond to the Personal Pronouns. They are of three Persons, Singular and Plural, and have Simple and Emphatic forms. They are declined with the Noun as follows:—

		SINGULAR	PLURAL
Simple	1.	**mo mhac** *my son*	**ar mac** *our son*
	2.	**do mhac** *thy son*	**bhur mac** *your son*
	3.	{ **a mhac** *his son* { **a mac** *her son*	**am mac** *their son*

Mo and **do** drop **o** before Nouns with a Vowel initial, and the fact is indicated by an apostrophe; **m'athair** *my father*, **d'each** *thy horse*. In the same position **a** *his* drops out; **'athair** *his father*, **'each** *his horse*—for **a athair**, **a each**. In no circumstances does **a** *her* fall out; but before Vowels it takes **h**; **a h-athair** *her father*, **a h-each** *her horse*.

The Vowels of **mo, do,** and **a** *his* are also dropped after Prepositions ending in a Vowel—even before Consonant initials; **do m' mhac** *to my son*, **le m' charaid** *with my friend*, **gu 'mhac** *to his son*; but it is desirable to retain **a** *his* wherever that is possible, as when it follows a dissimilar Vowel, **le a mhac** *with his son*, **ri a charaid** *to* or *against his friend*.

Ann and **ag** enter into composition with the Possessive Pronouns thus; **'nam, 'nad, 'nar, 'nur**; **'gam, 'gad, 'gar, 'gur**, etc.; **'nam cheann** *in my head*, **'nad laimh** *in thy hand*, **'nar duthaich** *in our country*, **'gam bhualadh** *at my striking*, **bha mi 'gam fholach** *I was hiding myself* (*at my hiding*). The combination with **ag** is only used before the Infinitive or Verbal Noun.

Ar and **bhur** have **n** before Vowels; **ar n-athair** *our father*, **bhur n-each** *your horse*, and **an** *their*, which is common to both genders, changes to **am** before labials, **an caraid** *their friend* but **am mac** *their son*.

	SINGULAR	PLURAL
Emphatic 1.	**mo mhac-sa** *my son*	**ar mac-ne** *our son*
2.	**do mhac-sa** *thy son*	**bhur mac-sa** *your son*
3. {	**a mhac-san** *his son*	**am mac-san** *their son*
	a mac-se *her son*	

The meaning and use of the Emphatic form is closely represented by laying emphasis on the Pronoun in English.

The Emphatic syllable is suffixed to the Noun, as shown; and if an Adjective or more than one Adjective follows the Noun, the augment is affixed to the last; **mo mhac beag-sa** *my little son,* **bhur tigh geal ùr-sa** *your white new house.*

Fein may combine with the Possessive as with the Personal Pronoun, but here it means *own*; **mo mhac fein** *my own son,* and if an Adjective or Adjectives follow the Noun, **fein** like the Emphatic augment is put last, **mo mhac maith fein** *my own good son.*

A RELATIVE PRONOUN relates to a Noun or Pronoun going before it in the sentence. **Eilean ris an abrar Patmos** *an island named (to which is said) Patmos,* **an laoch a thuit** *the hero who fell,* **am fear nach do thuit** *the man who did not fall,* **thoir leat na tha agad** *take with you all that you have.*

The Relative forms are **an, a, nach** and **na.**

The form **an,** which is for earlier **san,** is the historical form of the Relative. It changes to **am** before Labials. Mr. MacFarlane calls this form the Verbal Article and says 'That **an (am)** is a form of the same Article which is used before Nouns is proved by the fact that Prepositions like **le** and **ri** add an **s** when they come before it'—a very shrewd observation, even if the proof is not conclusive. The form of the Relative is the same as that of the Nominative and Accusative Neuter of the old Article, and it is interesting that old Greek grammarians speak of the fore-Article and the after-Article, the latter being the Relative, so recognising the kinship of function which the kinship of form indicated. The **s** of **leis** and **ris** really belongs to the Relative.

Regarding **a** of the modern language, though it does not appear to be a Relative historically, but stands for the verbal particle **do,** it will be an advantage to the learner to look upon it as equivalent to the English Relative; **am fear a (do)**

thuit *the man who fell,* **an té a (do) thainig** *the woman who came,* **an ni a (do) chi mi** *the thing which I will see.*

Nach which may be rendered *that . . . not* is the Negative Relative used as direct negation to the forms **an** and **a**; **eilean ris nach abrar Patmos** *an island that is not named P.,* **an laoch nach do thuit** *the hero who fell not.*

Na *that which* or *all which* resembles English *what* in that it has no antecedent, or contains it; **fhuair mi na dh'iarr mi** *I got what* or *that which* or *all that I asked.*

All the Relative forms except **a** may be governed by a Preposition; **ris an abrar** *to which is said,* **ris nach abrar** *to which is not said,* **ris na dh'iarr mi** *to what I asked,* so also **air an do thuit** *on which fell,* **gus nach tig e** *till he comes not,* **leis na fhuair mi** *with all I got.*

THE DEMONSTRATIVE PRONOUNS are **so** *this,* **sin** *that,* **sud** *yon,* or *here, there, yonder.* Though usually classed as Pronouns these words have three distinct uses—as Pronouns or in the position of a Noun, as Adjectives, and as Adverbs.

1. As Pronouns or in the position of a Noun; **tha so maith** *this is good,* **chi mi sin** *I (will) see that,* **bha sud milis** *yon was sweet.* After Prepositions **an so** *here,* **gun sin** *without that,* **mar sud** *like yon.*

2. As Adjectives limiting a Noun or Pronoun as regards place and time; **an duine so** *the man here = this man* close at hand, **na laithean sin** *those days = the days there* some time past, **na fir ud** *yon men = the men yonder* at a distance, **na laithean ud** *yon days,* now long past. So also **thainig i so** *she here has come = this she,* **dh'fhalbh iad sud** *they yon have gone = yon they,* or

those persons referred to as at a distance in time or place.

3. As Adverbs, usually without Verb expressed and coming first in the sentence; **so am fear** *here (is) the man*, **sin iad** *there they (are)*, **sud na tighean** *yonder (are) the houses*.

THE INTERROGATIVE PRONOUNS are **co, cia, ciod** which are indeclinable. **Co** *who, which* is used of persons and less freely of animals, **ciod** is used of inanimate things; **co am fear a bhuail mi** *who is the man that struck me*, **co an t-each a tha agad** *which is the horse that you have* = *what horse have you*, **co a thuit** *who fell*, **ciod a rinn thu** *what have you done*.

Cia is not used very often now as a Pronoun, **co** has superseded it almost entirely. In such expressions as **cia lion** *how many*, **cia meud** *how much*, **cia mar tha thu** *how are you* it is not a Pronoun but an Adjective or an Adverb.

The interrogative words **cionnas** *how*, **ceana** *whither*, **c'aite** *where* and **c'arson** *wherefore* embody the old word **co** (**ca, ce**) and a Noun; thus, **cionnas** = **ce indas** *what manner* or *how*, **ceana** = **ce ionadh** from **inad** *place*, **c' aite** = **ce aite** *what place* or *where*.

The form **gu dé** which is so often heard and which maintains itself despite the effort to make it **ciod e** is a genuine old Gaelic form **caté, coté**. Such an expression as **gu dé do bharail** *what is your opinion* is constantly heard where **ciod i do bharail**, the supposed more grammatical expression, is not very acceptable, and **ciod e do bharail** would be very disagreeable. The form **gu dé** is preferably used for animals instead of **co**; **gu dé an t-each a tha agad** *what horse have you*. The first syllable is usually dropped in speaking; as, **dé an t-each**.

F

Creud for older cret=**ce rét** *what thing* is now gone quite out of use.

Co with a Personal Pronoun asks a question without a Verb expressed, the accent being on the Pronoun; **co e** *who (is) he*, **co iad** *who (are) they*?

With the Masculine forms of the Third Singular of most Prepositional Pronouns **co** and **cia** enter into composition—**co** for persons and **cia** for things—and the accent is on the second word; **co air** *on whom*, **co uaidh a fhuair thu sin** *from whom got you that*? **Cia as a thainig thu** *whence (out of which place) have you come*? **Co ris a ghlaodh mi** *to whom did I call*? **Co leis** lit. *with whom* means *to whom belongs*; **co leis an cù** *whose is the dog.* **C' uime** for **cia uime** *about what* is used equivalent to *wherefore*.

The Simple Prepositions coming after **co** do not govern **co** but a succeeding Relative in such expressions as **co ris an glaodh mi** *to whom shall I call*, **co do 'n innis mi** *to whom shall I tell*, **co mu 'n labhair mi** *about whom shall I speak.* **Co** in this position retains the accent.

In the old language the closeness of the composition was recognised and the distinction was made between these two constructions, by writing the two words as one; thus, **coleis thu, coleis an cù,** but **co risan glaodh mi, co leisan tig mi** *with whom shall I come*—and this exactly represents the pronunciation of the present day.

It is important to observe that the forms of the Interrogative Pronouns are also those of the Relative Conjunctions *who, which, what.* For this reason any interrogative expression may become an objective clause in a sentence; **seall co e** *look who he (is)*, **cha'n'eil fhios co am fear a bhuail mi** *it is not known who struck me*, **am bheil thu cinnteach co a thuit** *are you sure who fell*, **cha'n'eil fios cionnas a thuit e** *it is not known how he fell*, **innis dhomh co leis an cù** *tell me who owns the dog*.

The same forms **co, cia, ciod** go to form the so-called INDEFINITE PRONOUNS **co air bith, co 'sam bith** or **co 'sa bith** *whoever*, **ciod air bith** *whatever*, **cia b'e air bith** *whosoever*.

The phrases **air bith, 'sam bith** limit the terms to which they are attached, like Adjectives; **fear 'sam bith** *any man*, **duine air bith** *any man*, **nì 'sam bith** *anything—at all*. The former expression **air bith** would seem to point to the Welsh **byd** and the Old Gaelic **bith** *the world* as the source of the word **bith** which is here used.

CHAPTER VI—OF VERBS

A VERB is a word which signifies to be, to do, or to suffer anything.

Gaelic Verbs may be divided into three classes as Regular, Irregular, and Defective.

REGULAR VERBS are such as have the common root of the word in all the moods and tenses; as, **buail—bhuail—buailidh** *to strike*.

IRREGULAR VERBS are such as have not a common root throughout; as, **rach—chaidh—theid** *to go*.

DEFECTIVE VERBS are such as have not all the parts, or only a few of the parts of the ordinary declension; as, **ars** *quoth*, **theab** *had almost*.

A Verb may be used Transitively, Intransitively Impersonally, or as Auxiliary to another Verb.

The Verb is TRANSITIVE when its action passes on to an object; as, **bhuail e am bord** *he struck the table.*

It is INTRANSITIVE when the action does not pass on to an object; as, **thuit a' chraobh** *the tree fell.*

A Verb is used IMPERSONALLY when it has no Personal Nominative. It always takes the form of the Third Person Singular of the tenses of the Passive in Gaelic; **ghuileadh leinn** *we did weep.*

The Verb in Gaelic is declined by Voices, Moods, Tenses, Numbers, and Persons.

The VOICES are two, Active and Passive.

The ACTIVE expresses what the subject *does* or *is*; as, **bhuail mi** *I struck*, **tha mi tinn** *I am sick.*

The PASSIVE expresses what the subject *suffers* or *is done to*; as, **bhuaileadh mi** *I was struck.*

The MOODS are five; the Indicative, the Negative and Interrogative, the Subjunctive, the Imperative, and the Infinitive.

The INDICATIVE is used in simple assertion; as, **tha mi** *I am*, **bhuail mi** *I struck*, **bithidh mi** *I shall be.*

The NEGATIVE is used in negative statements; as, **cha'n'eil mi** *I am not*, **cha bhuail mi** *I shall not strike*: and the INTERROGATIVE is used in asking a question; as, **am beil mi** *am I?* **am buail mi** *shall I strike?* The Negative and Interrogative Moods are alike.

For convenience the two names will not be given in Conjugation, only *Interrogative.*

The SUBJUNCTIVE expresses a condition, motive or

wish, etc. It is commonly used with the Conjunctions **na'm, mur, nach,** etc.; as, **mur buailinn** *if I would not strike*, **na'm bithinn** *if I would be*.

The IMPERATIVE expresses a desire in the First Person, a command in the Second Person, and permission in the Third; as, (1) **buaileam** *let me strike* (2) **buail** *strike* (3) **buaileadh e** *let him strike*.

The INFINITIVE is in all respects a Noun denoting the action or energy of the Verb, and is commonly preceded by a Preposition which marks the time of the action; as, **bualadh** *striking*; **ag bualadh** *a-striking*; **iar bualadh** *after striking*.

The forms of the Verb may be referred to also as Dependent or Independent according as they are such as do or do not depend on a preceding Particle; **ma thogas mi** *if I shall lift*, **togaidh mi** *I shall lift*, **cha'n fhaca mi** *I did not see*, **chunnaic mi** *I saw*.

The TENSES are Present, Past and Future; and each of these has four forms for the more precise indication of time, namely Indefinite, Inceptive, Progressive and Perfect; as,

	PRESENT.	PAST.	FUTURE.
Indef.	(wanting)	**bhuail mi**	**buailidh mi**
Incept.	**tha mi dol a bhualadh**	**bha mi dol**..	**bithidh mi dol**..
Progress.	**tha mi a' bualadh**	**bha mi a'**..	**bithidh mi a'**..
Perf.	**tha mi iar bualadh**	**bha mi iar**..	**bithidh mi iar**..

There is not in Gaelic, as there cannot be in any correct expression of exact thought, an Indefinite Present Tense.

The INDEFINITE Past and Future affirm an action which took place in some past time or will take place in the future, without any indication of the exact time at which it did, or will, take place; **bhuail mi** *I struck*—sometime, **buailidh mi** *I shall strike*—sometime.

The INCEPTIVE form of the Tenses states an action as about to be, or about to come into effect; as, **tha mi dol a bhualadh** *I am going to strike*, **bha mi dol a bhualadh** *I was going to strike*.

The PROGRESSIVE forms indicate an action in progress; as, **bha mi a' bualadh** *I was (at) striking*.

The PERFECT forms express that the action is, was, or will have been, just completed; as, **tha mi iar bualadh** *I am after striking* = *I have struck*.

The Indefinite Tenses are usually spoken of as the Simple Tenses, and the others—Inceptive, Progressive and Perfect—as the Compound Tenses.

The NUMBERS are two; Singular and Plural.

The PERSONS are three; First, Second and Third. The distinction of Number and Person takes place in only a few tenses; as, **bhuailinn, buaileam, buaileamaid** —*I would strike, let me strike, let us strike*.

The inflections of Verbs like those of Nouns are made by changes at the beginning and on the termination.

The changes on the termination of all Regular Verbs are made according to one model and by the same rules. But for the sake of stating some diversity in the *initial* changes it may be convenient to arrange the Verbs in two Conjugations.

The FIRST CONJUGATION comprehends those Verbs

which begin with a Consonant; as, **paisg** *fold*, **buail** *strike*.

The SECOND CONJUGATION comprehends those Verbs which begin with a Vowel or with f-pure; as **òl** *drink*, **ith** *eat*, **fàg** *leave*.

FORMATION OF TENSES

The root of the Verb is in the Second Singular of the Imperative; as, **buail** *strike*, **òl** *drink*. The rest of the Imperative has Personal terminations.

The following are the changes which in the several Tenses take place:—

	ON THE BEGINNING		TERMINATION	
	Consonants.	Vowels.		
Indic. Past	Aspiration	do as dh'		bhuail, dh' òl
Fut.			-idh	buailidh, òlaidh
Inter. Past	do+Asp.	do as d'		(an) do bhuail, d' òl
Fut.				(am) buail, (an) òl
Subj. Past	Asp. except [1]	do as dh'	-inn, etc.	bhuailinn, dh' òlainn
Fut.	Asp. except [2]	do as dh'	-as	(ma) bhuaileas, dh' òlas

PASSIVE VOICE

Indic. Past	Aspiration	do as dh'	-adh	bhuaileadh, dh' òladh
Fut.			-ar	buailear, òlar
Inter. Past	do+Asp.	do as d'	-adh	(an) do bhuaileadh, d' òladh
Fut.			-ar	(am) buailear, (an) òlar
Subj. Past	Asp. except [1]	do as dh'	-tadh	bhuailteadh, dh' òltadh
Fut.	Asp. except [2]	do as dh'	-ar	bhuailear, dh' òlar

CHANGES AT BEGINNING.—1. All Past Tenses are aspirated—except the Past Subjunctive after **an (am) nach, mur, gu'n, na'n.**

2. Future Tenses do not aspirate—except Future Subjunctive after **ged, ma, o'n,** and the Future Negative after **cha.**

3. Verbs with a vowel initial (and **fh**) have **do** before all Tenses except the Future Indicative and Interrogative. **Do** is always aspirated, excepting in the Past Interrogative. It drops **o** always in this position.

These changes are alike for Active and Passive.

CHANGES ON THE TERMINATION.—These are very simple and are shown above. The Past Subjunctive and the Imperative of the Active have personal and other terminations which should be referred to (p. 102).

The Passive has no personal terminations.

The Participle Passive is formed by adding **te** to the stem; **buailte** *struck*, or **ta** for correspondence, **pòsta** *married*.

It is very interesting to observe how the Participle has resisted the law of Vowel correspondence. The forms in **ta** were never numerous; they are now extremely few, so much so that it is comparatively safe with any verb to make the Participle in **te**; **òl**—**òilte** and even **òlte** rather than **òlta** *drunk*, so **tog**—**togte** *raised*, **croch**—**crochte** *hanged*, where we should look for **togta** and **crochta**. The approximate explanation is that in its older form the termination was **ithi** or **ithe,** and that the effect of the narrowed Consonant still remains and asserts itself.

The Infinitive or Verbal Noun is formed variously as follows:—

1. A considerable number have the Infinitive like the stem; as, òl *drink* and òl *drinking* or *to drink*, so fàs *grow*, ruith *run*.

2. Some form the Infinitive by dropping i of the stem; as, caill *lose* call, guil *weep* gul, ceangail *bind* ceangal.

3. Many add adh to the stem; as, aom *incline* aomadh, ith *eat* itheadh.

But of these some syncopate; coisin *earn* cosnadh, fosgail *open* fosgladh.

And some drop i before adding adh; fàisg *wring* fàsgadh, buail *strike* bualadh.

4. A few add amh and a few ail to the root; caith *spend* caitheamh, cum *hold* cumail.

5. A number of dissyllables in air add t; agair *claim* agairt, labhair *speak* labhairt.

6. A number of monosyllables add tinn and sinn; cinn *grow* cinntinn, faic *see* faicsinn.

But when the Vowel of the root is Broad tinn becomes tuinn for correspondence; fan *stay* fantuinn, bean *touch* beantuinn.

7. A few add ich and a few achd; beuc *roar* beucaich, glaodh *cry* glaodhaich, eisd *hearken* eisdeachd, casd *cough* casdachd.

8. A small number are irregular; eirich *rise* eirigh, tuit *fall* tuiteam.

9. Some have more than one form of the Infinitive; thig *come* tighinn or teachd, ceil *conceal* ceiltinn or cleith.

It will be an advantage before entering on the regular Conjugations to study the Verbs is and bi as well as certain 'Particles'—mostly Conjunctions—that are intimately connected with the forms of the Verb.

Is *(it) is*

Indicative Mood—*Present Tense*

is mi *it is I*   **is sinn** *it is we*
is tu *it is thou*   **is sibh** *it is you*
is e or **i** *it is he* or *she*   **is iad** *it is they*

Past **bu mhi, tu** *it was I, thou*, etc.

Interrogative Mood

Present **am mi, an tu** *is it I, thou?* etc.
Past   (**am**) **bu mhi, tu** *was it I, thou?* etc.

Subjunctive Mood

Present **ma's** (for **ma is**) **mi, tu** *if it is I, thou*, etc.
Past   (**na'm**) **bu mhi, tu** *if it were I, thou*, etc.

This is the whole of the Verb which, it will be observed, has only two essential forms, **is** for the Present and **bu** for the Past; yet a thorough study of it and of its relationship to other Verbs and Parts of Speech constitutes a most important and considerable part of Gaelic grammar. With **bi** it forms numerous interesting combinations which must have close attention. Before investigating these, however, it will be better to examine the words which for convenience have been called Particles. The Particles are used with **is** in the order in which they are classified—Interrogatives, Negatives, Conditionals—with their respective moods. **Na** cannot be used as the Verb has no Imperative. **Ma** is used with the Present, **na'm** with the Past. The Verb is not expressed in the Present Interrogative and Negative. The assimilation of Consonants in the Present Interrogative should be noticed.

PARTICLES

It has been thought advantageous to bring the following words together under this heading, but as the name is hardly at all applicable, or only applicable to a very small extent, it is hoped that it shall in no way mislead the learner. The words, which have their proper grammatical place and function explained in detail, may be conveniently classified as Interrogative, Negative, and Conditional; as follows,

I. INTERROGATIVE

1. **an (am)**   an cluinn thu mi *will you hear me?*
2. **nach** (*will*) *not* nach tig thu *will you not come?*

II. NEGATIVE

1. **na** (*do*) *not*   na buail e *do not strike him.*
2. **cha** *not*   cha bhuail mi e *I shall not strike him.*
3. **mur** *if not*   mur buail e mi *if he will not strike me.*
4. **nach** *that not* thubhairt e nach tigeadh iad *he said that they would not come.*
5. **gu'n** *that*   thubhairt e gu'n tigeadh iad *he said that they would come.*

III. CONDITIONAL

1. **ged** *though*   ged bha mi *though I was.*
2. **ma** *if*   ma bhitheas mi *if I shall be.*
3. **na'n** *if*   na'n robh mi *if I had been.*
4. **o'n** *since*   o'n bha mi *since, because, I was.*

I.—1. **An** is not translatable. It simply expresses Direct Interrogation. *Will* may be used for it.

2. **Nach** is used when a question is asked by Negative form, or Indirectly.

An the Primary form becomes **am** before Labials; but in the Past tense the initial being covered by **do** this change does not take place, excepting in the case of **bu** which does not take **do** before it.

Nach occurs here in two positions, as an Interrogative at the beginning of sentences, and as a Relative Negative at the beginning of a subordinate clause. This is the same form as that already met with in the Relative Pronouns and the usage here illustrates the double function which other Interrogatives have been seen to perform.

It is important to observe that **an** also has these two uses of Interrogation and Relation; so, these forms serve for Relatives and Interrogatives, and their signification is determined by their position in the sentence.

Ged nach *though not*, **o nach** *since not*, are also used; **ged nach tig mi** *though I shall not come*, **o nach tig thu** *since you will not come*. These always introduce a subordinate clause.

II.—1. **Na** is only applied to, and with, the Imperative, to form an Imperative prohibition; as **na buail mi** *strike me not*.

It usually takes **h-** before Vowels; as, **na h-ol sin** *drink not that*, **na h-abair sin** *say not that=do not say so*. This however is not very essential; there is not much excuse for it in speaking except perhaps when an open **a** follows, and there is less excuse for it in writing.

2. **Cha** it will be observed aspirates initial Labials and Gutturals, but not Dentals. **Cha** simply negatives the signification of the Verb; (**do**) **bhuail mi** *I struck*, **cha do bhuail mi** *I did not strike*. It becomes **cha'n** before

initial Vowels or **f-**pure; as, **cha bhuail mi** *I will not strike*, **cha'n ol mi** *I shall not drink*, **cha'n fhosgail mi** *I shall not open.*

The fact that it does not aspirate Dentals (**cha duin mi** *I shall not shut*, **cha seinn mi** *I will not sing*) is interesting and important; for it shows the abiding influence of a lost Dental **n**—the **n**, doubtless, which reasserts itself before initial Vowels—and it shows further that it is wrong to separate the **n** of **chan** as is usually done in writing. Some write it **cha'n**, some **cha-n** and others **cha n-**, all of which shows uncertainty, is troublesome, inelegant and wrong.

Mur, nach, and **gu'n** do not aspirate the following initial consonant.

3. **Mur** is said to take **h-** before Vowels, and in order to conform to this it becomes **mura**; as, **mura h-ol mi** *if I shall not drink*. But this again is manifestly not an important matter. **Mur ol mi** is quite easily spoken and is better in every way, even if the other were not so unreasonable as it seems to be. For, if **h-** is necessary with **mur** then is the change to **mura** not necessary, and not right; and if **h-** is not necessary with **mur** neither **mura** nor **h-** is excusable. But it must be remembered that the old form was **mani**=**ma** *if* **ni** *not*, and that in Irish it is still **muna.**

5. **Gu'n** becomes **gu'm** before Labials; **gu'n robh mi** *that I was*, **gu'm beil mi** *that I am*, **gu'm bi mi** *that I shall be.*

In the Present Subjunctive of **is** where the Verb is not expressed it becomes **gur**; **thubhairt mi gur e a thuit** *I said that he (it was) who fell.*

There does not appear to be any very good reason for separating **n** aṣ is done in writing. The practice can only be based on the assumption that **gu** is the primary form and that **n** is either an euphonic introduction or a fragment of a lately lost word. This is not however correct. The old form was **con** *e.g.* **conidbarat acorpu** and the modern **gu'n** plays exactly the same part **gu'n iodhbaradh iad an cuirp** *that they should sacrifice their bodies*. To say that it is desirable to have a form distinct from the preposition **gun** is no sufficient excuse if the variation introduces or even suggests an error.

The fact that **gu'n** does not aspirate any of the initial Consonants is conclusive against its being an old form ending in a Vowel.

It is interesting that though in its more common uses **gu'n** is not a Negative, yet its grammatical conduct is like that of the Negatives **nach** and **mur**. It is interesting especially because **gun** has still a negative usage in such idioms as **dh' iarr iad orm gun mi dh' fhalbh** *they asked me not to go away*, **bu duilich leam gun thu bhi ann** *I was sorry that you were not there*; but this usage may be referred to the Preposition **gun** rather than to the Conjunction.

III.—1. **Ged** presents some interesting difficulties. Stewart held that **ged** was the primary form and has the following important note on the point:—

'The Conjunction **ged** loses the **d** when written before an Adjective or a Personal Pronoun; as, **ge binn do ghuth** *though your voice be sweet*, **ge h-ard Iehobhah** *though high Jehovah be*.

'The translators of the Scriptures seem to have erred in supposing **ge** to be the entire Conjunction, and that **d** is the Verbal Particle **do**. This has led them to write **ge d'** or **ge do** in situations in which **do** alters the sense from what was intended, or is totally inadmissible. **Ge do ghluais mi** Deut. xxix. 19 is given as the translation of *though I walk* i.e. *though I shall walk* but in reality it signifies *though I did walk* for **do ghluais** is a past tense. It ought to be **ged ghluais mi.**

'So also **ge do ghleidh thu mi** Judg. xiii. 16, *though you detain me*, ought rather to be **ged ghleidh thu mi. Ge do ghlaodhas iad rium** Jer. xi. 11, *though they cry to me* is not agreeable to the Gaelic idiom; it ought rather to be **ged ghlaodhas iad rium** as in Hos. xi. 7.

'In **ge do dh' fheudainnse muinghin bhi agam** Phil. iii. 4, *though I might have confidence* the Verbal Particle is doubled unnecessarily, and is surely not according to classical precision. Let it be written **ged dh' fheudainnse** . . . and the phrase is correct.

'**Ged do 's eigin domh am bas fhulang** Mark xiv. 31, *though I must suffer death*; and **ge do tha aireamh chloinn Israel** Rom. ix. 27, *though the number of the children of Israel be* are wrong, for the present tenses **is** and **tha** never take **do** before them. **Ged is eigin** and **ged tha** are liable to no objection.

'At other times when **do** appeared indisputably out of place the **d** has been dismissed altogether contrary to the usual mode of pronunciation; as, **ge nach 'eil** where the common pronunciation requires **ged nach 'eil.** So **ged' nach duin' an t-aodach** *though the clothes be not the man* and **ged' nach biodh ann ach an righ** *though it were only the king*, in Macintosh's *Gael. Prov.* the **d** is correctly retained because such is the constant way of pronouncing the phrase.

'These faulty expressions which, without intending to derogate from the high regard due to such respectable authorities, I have thus freely ventured to point out seem to have proceeded from mistaking the constituent letters of the Conjunction in question. It would appear that **d** was originally a radical letter of the word that through time it came like many other Consonants to be aspirated and became by degrees in some situations quiescent. In Irish it is written **giodh.** This manner of writing the word is adopted by the translator of Baxter's *Call*. One of its compounds is always written **gidheadh**. In these the **d** is preserved though in its aspirated state. In Scotland it is still pronounced **ged** without aspirating **d** at all. These circumstances put together seem to prove that final **d** is a radical constituent of this word.'

Though this criticism was at the time acknowledged to be correct and necessary the error still continues with us, in writing **ge'd** and **ged'**. But even if the continuance of the error did not justify the reproduction of the criticism it would be deserving of attention as a good example of right reasoning within the limits of the light at that time available.

Ged however still presents some difficulties.

Why for instance if 'final **d** is a radical constituent of this word' why does it aspirate as it does all initial Consonants with the single exception of **bu** the Past tense of the Substantive Verb, and why this exception?

Why does it even aspirate the **do** of the Past and Future tenses of Verbs with a Vowel initial or **f**-pure; as, **ged dh' ol mi** *though I drank*, **ged dh' olas mi** *though I shall drink*—**ged dh' fhosgail mi** *though I opened*?

And why is the Adjective not aspirated after **ge**; **ge binn a sheinn i** *though she sang sweetly*, **ge dona an saor 's maith a shliseag** *though the carpenter is bad his shaving is good*?

In the older language this word, or perhaps better say these words, had several forms and different usages. **Ce, ci, cid, cit, cesu, cetu** are some of the older forms represented in the modern language by **ge** and **ged**.

That **ged** aspirates the initial Consonant of a Verb following seems to point towards a form like **cetu** ending in a vowel. **Ceto thoisegu iniriss (iress** *faith*)=modern **ged thoisicheadh iad an creidimh** *though they were beyond them in faith*. This shows the historical continuity and practical identity of **ceto** and **ged**, and explains the cause of aspiration.

The form **ge**, again, that is used before Adjectives does not cause aspiration and this points towards a form ending in a Consonant like **cid cit**. The old usage confirms this inference **cid maith cid olc, cid álind . . . cid bec cid már**=modern **ge maith ge olc, ge alainn . . . ge beag ge mòr** *however good or evil, beautiful, or small or great.*

The reason why **bu** is not aspirated after **ged** points in the direction of an old Vowel form like **ce** or **ci**. So it is found to be, **cipe** for mod. **ge bu e** *who he be* **cea bu gur aslige**=mod. **ged bu ghur** (*sore*) **an slighe** *though sore was their travel,* **cer bo rig in domain Nabgodon ruad**=**ged bu righ an domhain N. ruadh** *though red Nebuchadnezzar was king of the world,* **cearboligda lethan** =**ged bu ligda** (*beautiful*) **lethan** *though beautiful (and) broad.*

It is therefore apparent that **ged** before Verbs stands for **cetu** or **ceto**, before Adjectives for **cid** or **cit**, and before **bu** for a Vowel form **ci** or **ce**.

Gidheadh=**cid** *though,* **ed** *it* (*is*).

2. **Ma** aspirates the initial Consonant of a Verb following and it is used with the Past Indicative **ma bhuail mi** *if I struck,* the Future Subjunctive **ma bhuaileas mi** *if I shall strike,* and the Present and Past Indicative of the Verb **bi**—**ma tha mi** *if I am.*

3. **Na'n** seems to be complementary to **ma**; it is used where **ma** is not used—before the Past Interrogative of **bi**; **na'n robh mi** *if I was,* and before the Past Subjunctive of all Verbs; **na'n tiginn** *if I would come.* It does not cause aspiration.

Na'n becomes **na'm** before Labials **na'm bithinn** *if I would be,* **na'm paisginn** *if I would fold.*

The predecessor of **na'n** seems to have been **dian** *e.g.* **robad bethu dom dian chomalinn**=mod. **bu bheatha dhomh na'n** comhlionainn. From this it would appear that there is no good reason for separating the last **n** in writing; as, **na'n tiginn, na'm paisginn**. If anything should be separated it is the first **n**, for Zeuss conjectures that **dian** was formed from **do-an**, and it is **dan** to the present day in Irish.

It may be a help to show the usage of **ma** and **na'n** thus—

	WITH BI.	WITH CONS.-VERB.	WITH VOWEL-VERB.
Pres. Indic.	ma tha mi		
Past Indic.	ma bha mi	ma bhuail mi	ma dh' òl mi
Fut. Subj.	ma bhitheas mi	ma bhuaileas mi	ma dh' òlas mi
Past Subj.	na'm bithinn	na'm buailinn	na'n olainn
Past Inter.	na'n robh mi		

O'n is peculiar in that it causes aspiration of all aspirable initial Consonants following it—even of the Dentals which we should not expect to be aspirated after **n**. The fact however is that **n** is an intrusion in this position. **O** is the Conjunction and it is essentially the same in meaning and form as the Preposition **o**; as in, **o roscar ind anim frisin corp** = mod. **ona scar an t-anam ris a' chorp** *since the soul separated from the body.*

The form most commonly heard now is **ona** as here given which some grammarians have misunderstood. It is merely another natural effort to supply 'a felt want.' The aspiration of the Verb, which remains as the effect of an old Vowel-ending word, sought a Vowel sound to precede it—but as **on** does not end in a Vowel, **a** is added, hence **ona**. As the aspiration of the initial demands simple **o** the more correct way would be to do away with the intruding **n** which makes the **a** necessary. The practice is however too firmly established now to expect this correction, and besides there may be some excuse or even justification for the second syllable as compensation for a lost Particle **do** or **ro** as in the example given; **o ro scar.**

Bi *be*

INDICATIVE—*Present Tense*

PARTICLES

Conditionals
ged, ma, o'n

1. **tha mi** *I am*   **tha sinn** *we are*
2. **tha thu** *thou art*   **tha sibh** *you are*
3. **tha e, i** *he, she is*   **tha iad** *they are*

Past **bha mi, thu**... *I was*, etc.

None   *Fut.* **bithidh mi, tu**... *I shall be*, etc.

INTERROGATIVE MOOD

All Particles

Pres. (am) **beil mi, thu**... *am I*, etc.
Past (an) **robh mi, thu**... *was I* or *have I been*, etc.
Fut. (am) **bi mi, thu**... *shall I be*, etc.

SUBJUNCTIVE MOOD

Past **bhithinn, bhitheadh tu, e**... *I would be*, etc.

Conditionals   *Fut.* (ma) **bhitheas mi, tu**... *if I shall be*, etc.

IMPERATIVE MOOD

Na

1. **bitheam** *let me be*   **bitheamaid** *let us be*
2. **bi** *be (thou)*   **bithibh** *be ye* or *you*
3. **bitheadh e, i** *let him, her be*   **bitheadh iad** *let them be*

INFINITIVE **bith** *being*

The following Impersonal forms are in use. They come into the Compound tenses of the Passive to form the Inceptive and Progressive forms of expression.

	PRES.	PAST	FUT.
Indic.	thatar	bhatar	bitear
Interr.	(am) beilear	(an) robhar	bithear
Subj.	(ma) thatar	bhatar	bhithear

Thatar ag ràdh *it is (being) said,* **bhatar a' togail an tighe** *the house was being built,* **ma bhithear a' cogadh** *if there shall be fighting.*

A form in **s** is also used; **bhatas a' togail an tighe**. The Past Subjunctive Passive form **biteadh** is used impersonally; **na'm biteadh a' togail an tighe** *if the house had been (in process of) being built.*

NOTE.—The First Plural Past Subjunctive is **bith-e-amaid** and the other Persons not shown are like the Second Singular; and these are the terminations of the Past Subjunctive for all Verbs. **Bheil** loses **bh** after **cha, n** being restored; **cha'n'eil mi** *I am not.*

It is most important to observe and to thoroughly learn at this point that for all Verbs, in the Active and Passive

1. The Future Indicative takes no Particle before it.

2. The Imperative takes **na** only, and **na** is confined to this Mood.

3. The Present and Past of the Indicative and the Future of the Subjunctive take the Conditional Particles or Conjunctions **ged, ma, o'n**.

4. The tenses of the Interrogative-Negative Mood and the Past Subjunctive take all Particles;

Except (for this Verb alone) that the only Conditional used in the Interrogative Mood is **na'n** before **robh**. The form **ged robh mi** *though I was* seems exceptional.

The Past Subjunctive is aspirated after **cha, ged, o'n**.

Where **ma** is used **na'n** is not. See p. 175.

Is with bi

1. The Present tense form **is** combines with **bi** in the Present and Past Indicative and with the two tenses of the Subjunctive.

Is mi .. a tha .. a bha .. a bhitheas .. a bhitheadh —sona
It is I .. who am .. who was .. will be .. would be —happy

2. The Past tense form **bu** combines with the Past of the Indicative and Subjunctive; **bu mhi .. a bha .. a bhitheadh** *it was I .. who was .. would be.*

These combinations may take any of the Particles except **na**; **nach mi a tha** *is it not I who am,* **cha mhi a bha** *it is not I who was,* **mur mi a bhitheas** *if it is not I who shall be,* **gur mi a bhitheadh** *that it is I who would be,* **ged bu mhi a bha** *though it was I who was,* **na'm bu mhi a bhitheadh** *if it were I who would be.*

3. **Nach** whether used as Interrogative or Relative takes the tenses of the Interrogative-Negative Mood and the Past Subjunctive; **nach 'eil, nach robh, nach bi—mi** *am I not, was I not, shall I not be* **nach bithinn** *would I not be* **nach bitheadh tu—sona** *would you not be—happy?*

As Relative; **is mi .. nach 'eil** *it is I who am not,* **bu mhi .. nach robh** *it was I who was not,* **is mi .. nach bitheadh—sona** *it is I who would not be—happy.*

A great number of combinations, perhaps thousands can be formed by these two Verbs and the Particles. It will be a most profitable exercise to practise the making of them.

FIRST CONJUGATION
buail *strike*
ACTIVE VOICE—SIMPLE TENSES

Indicative Mood

SING.	PLUR.
Past **bhuail mi, thu, e** or **i**;	**sinn, sibh, iad** *I struck*, etc.
Fut. **buailidh mi, tu**, etc.	*I shall* or *will strike*

Interrogative Mood

SING.	PLUR.
Past **(an) do bhuail mi, thu**, etc.	*did I strike?*
Fut. **(am) buail mi, thu**, etc.	*shall* or *will I strike?*

Subjunctive Mood

Past **bhuailinn, bhuaileadh tu, e** or **i**;	**bhuaileamaid, bhuaileadh sibh, iad,** *I would strike*, etc.
Fut. **(ma) bhuaileas mi, tu**, etc.	*if I shall* or *will strike*

Imperative Mood

1. **buaileam** *let me strike*
2. **buail** *strike (thou)*
3. **buaileadh e** or **i** *let him or her strike*

1. **buaileamaid** *let us strike*
2. **buailibh** *strike ye*
3. **buaileadh iad** *let them strike*

Infinitive
bualadh *striking*

The signification of the Principal Tense forms is indefinite with regard to Time.

COMPOUND TENSES

INDICATIVE MOOD—*Present Tense*

Indef.   (wanting)
Incept.   **tha mi, thu,** etc.   **dol a bhualadh**
               I am going to strike, etc.
Progress.   **tha mi, thu..**   **a' bualadh**
               I am a-striking
Perf.   **tha mi, thu..**   **iar bualadh**
               I am after striking = *I have struck*

Past Tense

Indef.   **bhuail mi, thu,** etc.   *I struck,* etc.
Incept.   **bha mi, thu..**   **dol a bhualadh**
               I was going to strike
Progress.   **bha mi, thu..**   **a' bualadh**
               I was a-striking
Perf.   **bha mi, thu..**   **iar bualadh**
               I had struck

Future Tense

Indef.   **buailidh mi, tu,** etc.   *I shall or will strike*
Incept.   **bithidh mi, tu..**   **dol a bhualadh**
               I shall be going to strike
Progress.   **bithidh mi, tu..**   **a' bualadh**
               I shall be striking
Perf.   **bithidh mi, tu..**   **iar bualadh**
               I shall have struck

All the other Moods are formed in exactly the same way, from the forms of the Verb **bi** and the temporal phrases **dol a bhualadh,** etc., and it is not necessary to state them at length.

PASSIVE VOICE—SIMPLE TENSES

Indicative Mood

SING.	PLUR.

Past **bhuaileadh mi, thu, e** or **i**; **sinn, sibh, iad** *I was struck*, etc.

Fut. **buailear mi, thu**, etc.   *I shall be struck*

Interrogative Mood

Past (**an**) **do bhuaileadh mi, thu,** etc. *was I struck?*
Fut. (**am**) **buailear mi, thu,** etc.   *shall I be struck?*

Subjunctive Mood

Past **bhuailteadh mi, thu,** etc.   *I would be struck*
Fut. (**ma**) **bhuailear mi, thu,** etc. *if I shall be struck*

Imperative Mood

1. **buailtear mi** *let me be struck*
2. **buailtear thu** *be thou struck*
3. **buailtear e** or **i** *let him or her be struck*

1. **buailtear sinn** *let us be struck*
2. **buailtear sibh** *be ye struck*
3. **buailtear iad** *let them be struck*

Participle **buailte** *struck*

Tu is used in the Active Indicative Future and in the tenses of the Subjunctive; but it is never used in the Passive in which it is always **thu**.

COMPOUND TENSES

Indicative Mood—*Present Tense*

Indef.   **tha mi, thu ... buailte** *I am struck*
Incept.   **thatar ... a' dol 'gam bhualadh** *I am going to be struck*
Progres.   **thatar ... 'gam bhualadh** *I am being struck*
Perf.   **tha mi, thu ... iar mo bhualadh** *I have been struck*

Past Tense

Indef.   **bha mi, thu ... buailte** *I was struck*
Incept.   **bhatar ... a' dol 'gam bhualadh** *I was about to be struck*
Progres.   **bhatar ... 'gam bhualadh** *I was being struck*
Perf.   **bha mi, thu ... iar mo bhualadh** *I had been struck*

Future Tense

Indef.   **bithidh mi, tu ... buailte** *I shall be struck*
Incept.   **bitear ... a' dol 'gam bhualadh** *I shall be about to be struck*
Progres.   **bitear ... 'gam bhualadh** *I shall be (being) struck*
Perf.   **bithidh mi, tu ... iar mo bhualadh** *I shall have been struck*

And so on with the other Moods.

The Impersonal form may be used in the Perfect—and even preferably to the form given; **thatar iar mo bhualadh** *I have been struck.*

SECOND CONJUGATION

òl *drink*   fàg *leave*

Indicative Mood

Past dh' òl mi *I drank*   dh' fhàg mi *I left*
Fut. òlaidh mi *I shall drink*   fàgaidh mi *I shall leave*

Interrogative Mood

Past (an) d' òl mi *did I drink?* (an) d' fhàg mi *did I leave?*
Fut. (an) òl mi *shall I drink?* (am) fàg mi *shall I leave?*

Subjunctive Mood

Past. dh' òlainn *I would drink*   dh' fhàgainn *I would leave*
Fut. (ma) dh' òlas mi *if I shall drink*   (ma) dh' fhàgas mi *if I shall leave*

Imperative Mood

SING.   PLUR.
1. òlam *let me drink*   òlamaid *let us drink*
2. òl *drink (thou)*   òlaibh *drink (ye)*
3. òladh e, i *let him, her, drink* òladh iad *let them drink*

So *Sing.* fàgam, fàg, fàgadh e, i ;
   Plur. fàgamaid, fàgaibh, fàgadh iad.

Infinitive

òl *drinking*   fàgail *leaving*

As the only difference between this Conjugation and the First, which has been given fully, is altogether limited to the Changes on the Beginning and as these are the same for Active and Passive (p. 87) it is not necessary to state the Passive Voice; nor is it necessary to state the Compound Tenses, the method in these being the same for both Conjugations.

A Transitive Verb is said to Reciprocate or reflect when the Subject, or the Personal Nominative to the Verb, becomes the Object also of the verbal action. The word **fein** *self* is affixed to the Object; thus,

> **bhuail mi mi-fein** *I struck myself.*
> **bhuail thu thu-fein** *you struck yourself.*
> **bhuail se e-fein** *he struck himself.*

And so on through all Persons, Simple Tenses and Moods of the Active Verb.

In the Compound Tenses the Auxiliary Verb is, as usual, placed first; then follows the Personal Pronoun as its Nominative; then the Preposition **ag** abridged to '**g** in the Inceptive and Progressive Tenses, after which follows the Possessive Pronoun corresponding in person to that which is the Nominative to the Verb, and lastly the Infinitive which is the Noun to the Possessive Pronoun. **Mo** and **do** are here changed by metathesis and the substitution of one broad Vowel for another into **am** and **ad**. **Tha mi 'gam bhualadh fein** rendered literally is *I am at my own striking* that is *I am at (the) striking of myself*, equivalent to *I am striking myself.*

'The reciprocal **fein** is sometimes omitted in the Compound Tenses; as, **tha mi 'gam bhualadh** but it is generally retained in the Third Person to prevent ambiguity. **Tha e 'ga bhualadh** may mean *he is striking him* (another person) or *he is striking himself.* But **tha e 'ga bhualadh fein** is not ambiguous and can only mean *he is striking himself.*'—STEWART.

IRREGULAR

	ACTIVE—Indicative		Interrogative	
	Past	Future	Past	Future
			(an)	(an)
1. *To say*	thubhairt mi etc. *I said*	their mi *I shall say*	d' thubhairt mi *Did I say?*	abair mi *Shall I say?*
2. *To bear*	rug mi	beiridh mi	d' rug mi	beir mi
3. *To give*	thug mi	bheir mi	d' thug mi	tabhair mi
4. *To come*	thainig mi	thig mi	d' thainig mi	tig mi
5. *To reach*	rainig mi	ruigidh mi	d' rainig mi	ruig mi
6. *To go*	chaidh mi	theid mi	deachaidh mi	teid mi
7. *To hear*	chuala mi	cluinnidh mi	cuala mi	cluinn mi
8. *To see*	chunnaic mi	chi mi	faca mi	faic mi
9. *To do*	rinn mi	ni mi	d' rinn mi	dean mi
0. *To get*	fhuair mi	gheibh mi	d' fhuair mi	faigh mi

PASSIVE—

1. *Was said*	thuirteadh	theirear	d' thuirteadh	abairear
2. *Was born*	rugadh mi etc.	beirear mi	d' rugadh mi	beirear mi
3. *Was given*	thugadh mi	bheirear mi	d' thugadh mi	toirear mi
4. *Was come*				
5. *Was reached*	rainigeadh mi	ruigear mi	d' rainigeadh mi	ruigear mi
6. *Was gone*				
7. *Was heard*	chualadh mi	cluinnear mi	cualadh mi	cluinnear mi
8. *Was seen*	chunnacadh	chithear mi	facadh mi	faicear mi
9. *Was done*	rinneadh mi	nithear mi	d' rinneadh mi	deanar mi
0. *Was got*	fhuaradh mi	gheibhear mi	d' fhuaradh mi	faighear mi

VERBS

SUBJUNCTIVE		IMPERATIVE	INFINITIVE	PARTI-CIPLE
Past	*Future*			
(ged)	(ma)			
theirinn	their mi	abaiream abair	(ag) radh	
I would say	*If I shall say*	*Let me say*	*saying*	
bheirinn	bheireas mi	beiream beir	a' breith	
bheirinn	bheir mi	thugam thoir	a' tabhairt	
thiginn	thig mi	thigeam thig	a' tighinn	
ruiginn	ruigeas mi	ruigeam ruig	a' ruigheachd	
rachainn	theid mi	racham rach	a' dol	
chluinninn	chluinneas mi	cluineam cluinn	a' cluinntinn	
chithinn	chi mi	faiceam faic	a' faicinn	
dheanainn	ni mi	deanam dean	a' deanamh	
gheibhinn	gheibh mi	faigheam faigh	a' faotainn	
theirteadh	theirear			
bheirteadh mi	bheirear mi			beirte
bheirteadh mi	bheirear mi			tugte
ruigteadh mi	ruigear mi			ruigte
chluinnteadh mi	chluinnear mi			cluinnte
chiteadh mi	chithear mi			faicte
dheantadh mi	nithear mi			deante
gheibhteadh mi	gheibhear mi			faighte

Three factors co-operate in the formation of these Irregular Verbs—Roots, Prepositive Particles, and Accent. The Accent is the most disturbing element; it saves the part on which it rests and leads to the destruction of the part that it leaves. The Infinitive **dol**, for instance, is made up of the Particle **do** and the merest fragment l of a Verb which had forms **luid dolluid** *ivit.*

Faigh also is from a Particle **fo** with a root **gab** that still remains intact in the verb **gabh** *take*, but all that is left of the verb in **faigh** is the **g** and even that aspirated and scarcely heard.

Faic, in which **f** is an intrusion as it is in many other Gaelic words, is of exceptional interest, for it illustrates more than one of the processes which have operated in the language to determine the forms of the present day. It is from an old form **ad-cesi**, and from that to **aic** the following changes have taken place, but not necessarily in this order; (1) **s** of **esi** being vowel-flanked got aspirated and dropped out; (2) **d** became **c** by assimilation (as in English *account* for *adcount*) and therefore a form **acci**; (3) the **i** was thrown into the body of the word as the accent was, according to the method of the language, carried on to the first syllable. This is what Zeuss calls Infection of **a** by **i**. The result is **aicc** which with the prothetic **f** is the present form and which though written **faic** is yet pronounced as with double **c**.

It will be observed that the strengthening of the Particle by the advancing of the Accent is the most important factor in all these changes.

The Particles used in these Verbs are **ad, do, fo, ro,** and **to** which last is the accented form of **do**. The signification of these in composition is less or more remotely associated with their original meaning as Prepositions.

It is interesting to observe that a root **ber** is common to the first three of the Irregular Verbs, as if Gaelic had long ago recognised that *to say* or *to bear* testimony was *to give* oneself away. The Infinitive **radh** is another distinct root. **Rug** and **thug** have a common root **ucc** which signifies *to carry*— ro-ucc, to-ucc.

Excepting the Infinitives which have the roots **teg** and **reg**, the next two (4, 5) have **ic** *to come* and **anic** in common; so, **thainig**=to-ànic, **rainig**=ro-ànic, and **thig**=to-ic, **ruig**=ro-ic.

The next is most irregular. It has **rach** (reg) **chaidh** (cuad) **theit** (do-eit) and **dol** (do-luid)—four separate roots.

Cluinn has a root **clo** or **clu** throughout, the same as in **cluas** *an ear*; and **faic** has **ci**. **Chunnaic**=con and **aca**=adchi as already explained, with the accent carried on to **con**.

Dean which looks so irregular is very regular, from a root **gni** from older **gen**; **ruin**=ro-gni, **ni**=gni in which the pronunciation is important proof, **dean**=do-gni ?

The root **gab** already referred to, as well as a new root in **fhuair** (**ver**) occurs in the last Verb of the list and perhaps the root of **faotainn** is that met with in **theit**=do eit=do-eti.

The Verbs **tabhair, abair, faic, faigh** have another form in Past Subj. beside that shown. It is derived from the theme (Second Imperative) and is used after Interrogative and Negative Particles. It is **ged bheirinn** but **an toirinn** *would I give*, **ma theirinn** *if I would say* but **na'n abairinn, o'n chithinn** *since I would see* but **nach faicinn** *would I not see,* **ged gheibhinn** *though I would get* but **mur faighinn** *if I would not get.*

Tabhair has also **tugainn**; **na'n tugainn** *if I would give.*

The Passive has parallel impersonal forms; **an toirteadh** *would (it) be given* and **an tugteadh, ma theirteadh** *if it would be said* but **na'n abairteadh, o'n chiteadh** *since it would be seen* but **nach faicteadh** *would it not be seen,* **ged gheibhteadh** *though it would be got* but **mur faighteadh** *if it would not be got.*

Two verbs have a form in **s** also in the Past Indicative Passive; **chualas** (*it*) *was heard* and **chunnacas** (*it*) *was seen*. These forms are used in preference to the regular forms.

Beir and **tabhair** have the same form in the Past Subjunctive but **bheirteadh** of the latter is impersonal and needs a Prepositional Pronoun after it; **bheirteadh mi** *I was born* but **bheirteadh dhomh** *it was given to me.*

AUXILIARY VERBS

It has been already shown how **bi** *be* is used as an Auxiliary in the declension of all Verbs. There are two other Verbs which are occasionally employed in a similar capacity, the one with an Active the other with a Passive effect; namely, **dean** *do* or *make* and **rach** *go*.

The Simple tenses of **dean** combined with the Infinitive of any Verb, correspond to the English Auxiliary *do, did*. It sometimes adds to the emphasis but not to the sense; **rinn mi suidhe** *I made sitting=I sat* or *did sit*, **ni mi seasamh** *I shall make standing=I shall stand*, **dheanainn gul** *I would make weeping=I would weep*. These are with Infinitives of Intransitive Verbs.

With the Infinitives of Transitive Verbs; as, **rinn e bualadh** *he made striking* or *he did strike=he struck*, the object is indefinite, but with a Possessive Pronoun it is made definite, **rinn e mo bhualadh** *he made my striking=he struck me*, **ni thu mo ghearradh** *you will cut me*, **dean do gharadh** *warm thyself*.

The Simple tenses of **rach** combined with the Infinitive of a Transitive Verb correspond to the Passive Voice of the Verb; **chaidh mo bhualadh** *my striking went=I was struck*, **theid mo mharbhadh** *my killing will go=I shall be killed*.

It should be noticed that the First Singular and Plural of the Past Subjunctive—and such Imperative forms as have the Personal termination—drop the termination in this connection; so, **rachadh mo bhualadh** *I would be struck*—not **rachainn**, **rachadh ar bualadh** *we should be struck*—not **rachamaid**.

Where **dean** or **rach** is combined with the Infinitive of a Transitive Verb as shown, the Possessive may give place to the corresponding Emphatic Personal Pronoun with the Preposition **do**, here smoothed down to **a**, before the Infinitive; **rinn e mise a bhualadh** *he struck me*, **ni thu mise a ghearradh** *you will cut me*, **dean mise a gharadh** *warm (thou) me*. Before a Verb of the Second Conjugation the Preposition is dropped for obvious reason; **rinn e mise fhàgail** *he left me*, **ni e thusa àrdachadh** *he will exalt thee*.

In like manner a Noun or a Demonstrative Pronoun may take the place of this Personal Pronoun; **rinn e Ian a bhualadh** *he struck John*, **chaidh sin a ghearradh** *that was cut*, **dean sin òl** *drink (thou) that*.

The Future forms **faodaidh** *may* and **feumaidh** *must* with the Past Subjunctive forms **dh' fhaodainn** *I might* and **dh' fheumainn** *I must needs* or *it was necessary for me*, may be used as Auxiliaries in all respects as **dean** and **rach** have been seen to be used; **faodaidh mi seasamh** *I may stand*, **feumaidh mi do bhualadh** *I must strike you*, **dh' fhaodainn esan a bhualadh** *I might have struck him*, **dh' fheumadh e so òl** *it was necessary for him to drink this*. **Fimiridh** is in meaning, inflection, and usage exactly like **feumaidh**.

A number of Gaelic idiomatic expressions have a meaning nearly equivalent to what is expressed in English by a single verb; **is urrainn domh** *it is possibility to me* in English *I can*, **is toigh leam** *it is choice with me* = *I like*, **is mòr agam** *I esteem*.

These idioms are composed of the tenses of **is** and **bi** with a Noun or Adjective and a Prepositional Pronoun. (See Idioms, p. 173.) The idiom in **is** is Transitive, that in **bi** is Intransitive; **is beag orm buaireas** *I dislike strife*, **tha cuimhne**

againn air an là sin *we remember that day*, **bithidh fiughair agaibh ri Seumas** *you shall expect James*.

The following Verbs are DEFECTIVE, namely:

Ars *said* which has no inflection; **ars iad** *said they*, **ars Ian** *said John*. When a Personal Pronoun is Nominative it is most frequently used in the Emphatic form; **ars mise** *said I*, **ars thusa** *said thou*, **ars iadsan** *said they*.

Theab *had almost* has no inflection but has a Passive or Impersonal form **theabadh**; **theab mi tuiteam** *I nearly fell* or *had almost fallen*, **theabadh mo mharbhadh** *I was nearly killed* or *it was almost my killing*.

The following four Verbs are only used in the Second Imperative:

Feuch *behold* and **feuchaibh** *behold ye* (not **feuch** *try*).
Siuthad *proceed* and **siuthadaibh** *proceed ye*.
Tiugainn *come* and **tiugainnibh** *come ye*—along with me.
Trobhad *come hither* and **trobhadaibh** *come ye hither*.

It should be observed that all the Principal Tenses are now Aorist or Indefinite Tenses and that there is no particular form of the Verb for the expression of Definite time, hence the great importance of a thorough study of the forms of expression which have been arranged under the Compound Tenses. The Principal tense forms are put in series with the others to give a clear idea of their sequence.

There is no Present Tense form in the Gaelic Verb; that is, no Indefinite Present Tense. It has been lately discovered that this is the case with the Classic languages also. The Future Tense form is used for the Present; **chi mi sin** *I see that* lit. *I shall see that*, **fuaighidh mi so** *I sew this* lit. *shall sew*.

The Present has no existence in reality. It is only the

metaphysical line which separates the Past from the Future, so that any conceivable Present must be a realisation of, or won from, the Future. The language therefore with great beauty and precision uses the Future form for the expression of Present time, or rather for the expression of continuous Present, movable, and always moving into the Future. **Chi mi** *I see* is Future as truly when applied to the present day or hour or minute or second of time as when it means *I shall or will see*—to-morrow or next year or some time.

It is not now necessary as it was in Stewart's time to argue at length that the Infinitive is in every respect a Noun expressing the energy or action of the Verb, for which reason grammarians call it *Nomen Actionis,* or a Noun of Action. It has distinction of Gender, **an t-òl** *the drinking,* **an labhairt** *the speaking;* it is governed in the Genitive by another Noun **miann an òil** *desire of drink(ing);* it governs a Genitive, **bualadh nam bas** *striking of the palms (hands);* it can be the Subject or Object of a finite Verb, **ni ceangal cinnteach** *binding will make sure,* **rinn e fuasgladh oirnn** *he delivered us* lit. *be made unbinding on us,* and it may be governed by a Preposition, **o eiridh na grèine** *from (the) rising of the sun.* Stewart's observation that this part of the Verb being declined and governed like a Noun bears a closer resemblance to the Latin Gerund than to the Infinitive is quite pertinent and correct.

The usage of the Infinitive after certain Prepositions must be closely studied. The Infinitive with **ag** forms an equivalent to the English Present Participle, and with **iar** to the Perfect Participle; **ag òl** *(at) drinking,* **a' bualadh** *(at) striking,* **iar teachd dha** *he having come = after he had come* lit. *after coming (was) to him.* **Do** becomes **a** in this position, and is very near to Lat. *ad.* **Chaidh e a bhualadh** *he went (for) to strike,* ad *captandam vulgaris* **a ghlacadh na gràisg**. **Ri** is almost equal to a Verb **bha e a' deanamh bròin** is better expressed by **bha e rì bròn** *he was sorrowing* lit. *he was making sorrow.*

The other Prepositions have their simple usage **gu, mu, romh . . eiridh na grèine** *to, about, before . . the rising of the sun.*

CHAPTER VII—OF ADVERBS

An Adverb considered as a separate part of speech is a single indeclinable word significant of time, place, manner, degree, or any other circumstance which modifies the action of a Verb or qualifies the attribute signified by an Adjective; as, **thainig iad cheana** *they have already come,* **bha iad shios** *they were below,* **labhair e gu gasda** *he spoke well,* **bithidh fonn oirnn daonnan** *we shall be happy always,* **thig e am maireach** *he will come to-morrow,* **tha sin gle mhaith** *that is very good,* **bha an latha anabarrach breagh** *the day was exceedingly fine.*

The number of simple Adverbs in Gaelic is small, that is of Adverbs formed of single words; but Adverbial Phrases made up of two or more words are numerous; as **mu'n cuairt** *around,* **an comhair a chuil** *backwards =towards his back,* **bun os ceann** *heels over head, topsy turvy,* **uigh ar n-uigh** *gradually,* **mar an ceudna** *likewise,* **air chor eigin** *somehow.*

Almost all Adjectives may be made Adverbial Phrases indicative of Manner by prefixing **gu**; as, **fior** *true* **gu fior** *truly,* **maith** *good* **gu maith** *well,* **dona** *bad* **gu dona** *badly,* **cinnteach** *certain* **gu cinnteach** *certainly.* After **gu** before Vowels h '*in hiatu*' occurs; as, **gu h-ard** *highly* or *above,* **gu h-iosal** *lowly* or *below.* But perhaps this h stands for s of the original Preposition **cos**, which in this Vowel-flanked position would have got aspirated and disappeared as such.

When two or more Adverbs of this class come together, **gu** is used for the first only; **labhair e gu cruaidh, ceann-laidir crosta** *he spoke hard, headstrong, cross.* Similarly, when the Adverbial Adjective is qualified by **ro, glé, fior**, etc., these words are not repeated, **labhair e gu ro chruaidh, cheann-laidir, chrosta.** But if a Conjunction intervenes **gu** and **ro**, etc., are repeated; **labhair e gu ro chruaidh agus gu ro chrosta.** And for emphasis the qualifying words may be used in each phrase; **gu ro naomh, gu ro ghlic, agus gu ro chumhachdach** *most holy, most wisely, and most powerfully.*

Adverbs of this class take the Comparative also; as, **rinn e sin gu maith** *he did that well*, **rinn e sin na b' fhearr** *he did that better*; **labhair e gu cinnteach** *he spoke certainly=with certainty*, **labhair e na bu chinntiche** *he spoke more certainly.*

There is no direct Superlative of this form of expression. The Superlative idea is removed from the Action to the Agent; **bu e a b' fhearr a rinn sin** *he it was who did that best*, **bu e bu chinntiche a labhair** *he it was who spoke most certainly =with most certainty*, **bu e bu shoilleire a labhair** *he it was who spoke most clearly.*

This **gu** is for the old Preposition **cos** which took the form **co** in this connection *e.g.* **cohopin, coleir cumenicc** and **cominic** (Kal.) *suddenly, altogether, often.* It is akin to Latin *usque* of which the old form was perhaps *quos-que* and to Greek κατά which similarly went to form Adverbs in this way κατά μικρόν **gu beag** *paulatim* **a bheag 's a bheag.**

Some Adjectives may be used adverbially without taking **gu**; **chaidh e direach, claon, cam, crasgach, gobhlach**, etc., *he went straight, astray, crooked, crosswise, astride.* So also **fada** *long* **goirid** *short.*

A few Nouns expressive of time and distance may be used adverbially; **là dhomh bhi sealg** *on a day when hunting.*

The following list contains the Simple Adverbs as well as other groups of associated Adverbs in common use.

SIMPLE ADVERBS

Of Time

Present—**nis** or **a͏nis** *now*

Past—**cheana** *already*	*Future*—**fhathast** *yet*
roimhe *before*	**rìs** or **a rìs** *again*
riamh *ever*	**feasd** *for ever*
cian *ages past*	**chaoidh** *ages to come*
Indefinite—**daonnan** *always*	**minic** *frequently*
fòs *still, yet*	**ana-minic, ainmic** *seldom*
idir *at all*	**'nuair** *when*

Interrogative—**cuin** *when?*

Of Place

The first three may be arranged according as they express a state of rest or of motion.

REST	MOTION TO	MOTION FROM
shios *below*	**a sios** *down*	**a nios** *up from below*
shuas *above*	**a suas** *up*	**a nuas** *down from above*
thall *on the other side*	**a null** *over to the other side*	**a nall** *over from the other side*

Bhos *on this side* has no forms of Motion.

n-ear, n-iar, tuath, deas *east, west, north, south*
an so, an sin, an sud, *here, there, yonder*
mar so, mar sin, mar sud *like this, like that, like yon* = *thus, so, as*
an diu, an dé, am maireach *to-day, yesterday, to-morrow*
a stigh, am muigh or **a steach, am mach** *within, without.*

Phrases in **air** (old ar-e aspirating), **air dheireadh** *behind*, **air thoiseach** *before*, **air thùs** *in the beginning*.

Like **roimhe** are other forms of the Third Masculine of the Prepositional Pronouns **ann, as, fodha, leis ris, thairis**; **cha 'n** 'eil e ann *he is not there*, chaidh e as *he escaped*, chaidh e fodha *he went under*, thainig e thairis *he came across.*

Far *where* is the Preposition for. It governs the word following like other Prepositions ; far an robh mi *where I was.*

CHAPTER VIII—PREPOSITIONS

PREPOSITIONS are words used to show the relation of one Noun or Pronoun to another, in a sentence; and they are so called because they are placed before the word which is the object of the relation ; as, tha e aig an tigh *he is at the house*, chaidh e do 'n bhaile *he went to the town.*

The following are the Prepositions:

aig, ag *at*
air *upon*
(ar) *beside, against (apud)*
ann, anns *in*
a, as *out of*
de *of, from*
do *to, into*
eadar *between, both*
(fa) *upon*
fo *under*
gu, gus *towards*

gun *without*
iar *after*
le, leis *with*
mar *like to*
mu *about*
o, ua *from*
os *above*
ri, ris *to, against*
roimh *before*
seach *past*
tar *over*

troimh, tre *through*

All Prepositions having the form in s ended originally in s or in some other Consonant, the effect of which is still felt in that the Noun following is not aspirated— that is, it remains in the older form which previous presence of the preceding final Consonant secured. This is a very interesting example of the influence of a letter remaining long after the disappearance of the letter itself.

Other Prepositions also used to have the form in **s**. **Air** *upon* had it and **con** *with*, **iar** *after*, **ren** *before*, **tar** *across* and **tre** *through*; **cach dia forsindaltoir** *every god upon the altar*, **tarsnadeo** *through the gods*. This always occurred when the Preposition combined with the Article or Relative. The Article originally had initial-**s**; so, in the cases of such Prepositions as did not end in **s** we may infer that the terminal-**s** form came through assimilation to the initial of the Article. Thus, the Prepositions **in, co(th), la(th), fri(th)**, in composition became **is, cos, las, fris**; as **issind rigthig** *in the king('s) house*, **cossin tech** *to the house*, **lassin druid** *with the magician*, **frissin n-grein** *against the sun*.

The forms in **s** still retained, are used before the Article, the Relative Pronouns, and the Adjective **gach**; **anns an tigh** *in the house*, **am fear leis an robh mi** *the man with whom I was*, **thainig iad as gach aite** *they came from every place*.

Some Prepositions, **air, ann, ar, fo, gu,** and **mu** in the old language governed sometimes the Dative and sometimes the Accusative—the Dative when signifying a state of rest, and the Accusative after a Verb of Motion; **forsna feraib** *upon the men*, **digail for pecthachu** *revenge upon sinners*. Others governed the Dative only, **o, as, aig, de, do, ren,** and **iar**, with **is** and **os** which are now almost gone out of use; and the rest, **le, ri, tre, seach, gun** and **eadar** governed the Accusative only; **as for n-gnimaib** *out of your deeds*, **o chianaib** *from of old*,

dona mnaib *to the women,* **fri apstalu** *to apostles,* **cen na niulu** *without the clouds.*

The Prepositions **ar, gun, os,** and **seach** do not now combine with the Personal Pronouns though they used to do so—**ar** freely, **cen** not so freely, **os** only in a few instances and **seach** as appears only in the Third Person Plural, **seccu** *past* or *beyond them.*

On the other hand while combinations with **fo, ren, tar, tre** were few and with **oc** only in the Third Person Singular these in the modern language combine with all Personal Pronouns freely, **fodham, romham, taram, tromham, agam,** etc.

The combinations formed by the Personal Pronouns with the Prepositions which governed the two cases had as a rule two forms; as, **indib** and **intiu** *in them,* **forib** and **forru** *upon them,* but in the modern language the Accusative form alone is retained. There are only two Dative forms of the Third Person Plural, and they are of the Dative class **de** and **do**—**diubh** and **doibh.**

Ag, aig, more exactly rendered, means *near to* or *close up to.* The older form was **oc** sometimes written **ac** and very rarely **ic.** From the form **ucc** which occurs in *Tir.* ii. Whitley Stokes says that it may come from *oncva* = Goth. *nehva* and English *nigh.*

This was the root in **ocus** *near* and **ocus** *and* which are now written **fagus** and **agus**; i cein ocus i n-ocus = an cein agus am fagus (Patrick's Hymn), besu ocus besu chian = biodh e fagus biodh e cian (Imram Brain).

The simpler form **ag** is still used before the Infinitive or Verbal Noun, and in composition with the Personal Pronouns.

Air appears to be misunderstood. It is usually translated *on* or *upon* but in many positions this rendering is impossible; *e.g.* **tha i air chall** *she is upon loss* for *is lost*, which is not sense. Then again though this Preposition is said not to cause aspiration by rule, there are very many instances in which it does; **air dheireadh** *behind*, **air thoiseach** *before*, **air chionn** *in readiness for*, and it may be observed that where it causes aspiration it cannot be translated *upon*—as in the instance given, **air chall**. This indicates an exceptionally distinct difference between the one usage and the other for which there must be some reason. The reason seems to be that **air** in the modern language represents or rather misrepresents two old Prepositions **ar** and **for**.

Ar meant *before, against* or *beside* and was not unlike the Latin *apud* and the Greek παρὰ; and it caused aspiration of the word following because it originally ended in a Vowel and had the form **are** or **ari**; **ar thùs** *at the beginning*, **ar guin ar guasacht ar gabud a Crist for do snadud dùn** = **an aghaidh guin guasacht** (*trouble*) **'us gabhaidh a Christ thoir do shnadadh** (*protection*) **duinn** (Patrick's Hymn)—which shows the usage of **ar**, but not the aspiration in this case, which must be esteemed exceptional.

For on the other hand meant *upon* and was nearly the same meaning as Latin *super* and Greek ὑπέρ; and it did not cause aspiration. This **for** is the **air** proper of the modern Grammar.

Ar used to combine with the Personal Pronouns but does not do so now. The old forms were **airium, erut, airi**, etc., and it is not unlikely that this combination explains the form **air** *on him*, of the modern Third Person Singular Masculine which is different from all the other forms of the combination with **for**—(f)orm (f)ort (f)air; (f)oirnn (f)oirbh (f)orra. The f has fallen out in the modern language.

There seems therefore to be sufficient reason for restoring **ar** to its proper position, and it is to be hoped that Gaelic writers will recognise the propriety and the duty of using the right form in the right place, for by so doing they will strengthen the language and simplify its study by doing away with an extensive and troublesome and incorrect 'exception.'

Ann is very often written double; **ann an eolas** *in knowledge*, but it is doubtful if this is commendable or correct. It seems to be writing the Preposition not only double but even triple for the double **n** of **ann** seems to be already a repetition, so that **ann an** is not unlike what is sometimes heard in English *he took it off of me*.

The final **n** or **nn** is changed to **m** before Labials; **am measg** *in midst, among*, **ann am meas** *in esteem*, **ann am buaidh** *in victory*—but **am meas, am buaidh**, would seem to be from every point of view more desirable.

Before the Article and the Relative and **gach** the form in **s** is used; **anns an toiseach** *in the beginning*, **an cor anns am beil e** *the condition in which he is*, and in this position **ann** is dropped—in speaking, especially—the s alone being retained; **'s an toiseach, an cor 's am beil e.**

In was the old form of this Preposition, and with the Article it became **is** and **iss** (for **ins**); **issingemrud**=**anns a' gheamhradh, issatech**=**anns an teach** from which **isteach** *within*, and so also the peculiar forms **is tir**=**anns an tir** and those of the modern language **as t-earrach** *in the spring*, **as**

t-fhoghar *in the autumn*—**bidh gille aig an fheannaig as t-fhoghar** *the hoody-crow will have a servant in the autumn.*

A, as means *out of* or *from the inside of*, as against **o** which means simply *from* or *from the outside of*. The early form was **ass** and **as**, as it is still preserved in the Prepositional Pronouns and before Possessives—**asam, asad,** etc., **as mo thigh** *out of my house*, **as do chuidsa** *from (out of) your portion*. The effect of **s** though lost now is still felt in that the form **a** does not cause aspiration of a succeeding initial Consonant.

A, as corresponds to the Latin *e, ex* and to Greek ἐξ as **o** to *a, ab, abs* and ἀπὸ meaning *from out of* and *from*; and these respectively are opposed by **do** *into* and **gu** *towards* which correspond to εἰς and πρὸς and to Latin *in* (with Accusative) and *ad*. Stokes thinks that **do** is philologically related to *do* in Latin *endo* and to *de* in such Greek forms as οἰκόν-δε. The usage of these Prepositions is well illustrated in Luke ii. 4. **Agus chaidh Ioseph mar an ceudna suas** *o* **Ghalile,** *a* **baile Nasaret** *do* **Iudea,** *gu* **baile Dhaibhidh** ' and Joseph also went up *from* Galilee *out of* the city of Nazareth *into* Judea *to* the city of David.'

De used to be more frequently written as **di** and it is in this form we find it in composition. In modern Gaelic it has been confounded with **do** to so great an extent that in some parts it has been practically lost. It is to be observed that **de** and **do** are the only Prepositions which retain the old Dative Plural form in the composition with Personal Pronouns—**diubh, doibh.**

The Preposition **do,** like the Verbal Particle and the Possessive Pronoun of the same form, loses **o** before a Vowel and the Consonant **d** is aspirated, thus **dh' Albainn** *to Scotland.*

It is also preceded by the Vowel **a** when it follows a Consonant; as, **a dol a dh' Eirinn** *going to Ireland*. This **a** seems to be nothing else than the Vowel of **do** transposed, just as the letters of the Pronouns **mo, do** are in certain situations transposed and become **am, ad.** In this situation perhaps it would be advisable to join the **a** to the **dh**, thus **a dol adh Eirinn.** This would rid us of one superfluous **a** that appears as a separate inexplicable word.

The same remarks apply to **de** ; for instance, **armailt mhòr de dhaoinibh agus a dh' eachaibh** *a great army of men and of horses*, **lan do (de) reubainn agus a dh' aingidheachd** *full of ravening and of wickedness* (Luke xi. 39).

Do, as has been already observed, often loses **d** altogether and is written **a**; as, **dol a Dhuneidin** *going to Edinburgh*. When the Preposition is thus deprived of its articulation and only a feeble obscure Vowel sound is left, another corruption very naturally follows, and this Vowel also is discarded not only in speaking, but even in writing; as, **chaidh e Dhuneidin** *he went to Edinburgh*, where the Noun appears in its aspirated form without any word to govern it.

Eadar corresponds with Latin *inter*. It used to be written **itir, eter** and **etar**—**n** having fallen out before **t** as it does by rule, *e.g.* **ceud** *a hundred* is older **cét** = Lat. *cent*, so **deud** *a tooth* was **dét** = *dent*. In the now extinct Cornish it was **intre** and **yntre** as in **yntrethon** = **eadaruinn, yntretha** = **eatorra** *between us—them*. In the old language it always governed the Accusative and it does so in the modern language also; **eadar a' chraobh agus a' chlach** *between the tree and the stone*. It does not cause aspiration; **eadar clach 'us craobh** *between a stone and a tree*.

Sometimes it means *both* in which condition it takes the aspirated form of the noun; **eadar cheann 'us chasan** *both head and feet,* **eadar shean 'us òg** *both old and young.* **Eadar** in this connection will not admit the Article between itself and the Noun, and it governs the Genitive, from which fact it might be inferred that it was a Noun something like **timchioll, feadh**, etc.

In the light of what has been observed with regard to the double signification and usage of the Preposition **air**, this double meaning and different grammatical conduct of **eadar** is particularly interesting. Analogy would lead us to suspect that the modern **eadar** represents two old words; and we might reason that **eadar** *both* was at one time a word ending in a Vowel—because it aspirates a following initial Consonant. The only word which seems open to suspicion is **echtar** an old Preposition corresponding to Latin *extr-a*. It is met with in old Welsh as **eithir** which is very like the Gaelic **eadar**, especially like the old forms given above. The use of **echtar** seems to have been very limited even in old Gaelic. It appears to have been lost to Cornish and Armorican even before the time of their earliest records, for it is not met with in these dialects. If the suspicion then be correct regarding the kinship of the word, it must be concluded that this influence of **eadar** *both* is the evidence and effect of an extremely old and long lost form of the word which had ended in a Vowel. But however interesting this line of reasoning may appear it must be distinctly understood to be altogether speculative, and only put forward for consideration. It is either in this way or in the direction of esteeming **eadar** a Prepositional Noun that the truth seems to lie.

Fa is peculiar. It has no history. It is not found in the old language except in a few phrases **fa di, fa tri, fa dess no fa thuath** which Zeuss renders *ad dextram vel sinistram* and regarding which he adds '*ubi* **fa**=**ba** *si non est pro praep.* **fo**.' It is most commonly met with as a variant of **fo**. In the Prologue to the *Calendar of Oengus* l. 86 it means *under whom* or *by whom* = **foan**; **Hiruath ocus Pelait fa rochés ar fiadu (fiada** a name for God) *Herod and Pilate by whom our Lord suffered.* It does not seem to be correct or necessary even in the few phrases in which the modern language uses it, like **fa chomhair** *in the presence of*, **fa leth** *apart, individually, singulatim,* **fa dheoidh** *at last.* **Fa leth** is always written **fo leth** in the old language and **fa dheoidh** as **fo deud.**

Fo according to Stokes has had origin in this way 'from Sanskrit *upa* Greek ὑπό, the *p* being ejected and the initial *u* = *v* becoming strengthened to *f*,' as there is a tendency *e.g.* **fion** = vinum *wine* οἶνος.

It is interesting to notice that **fo** *under* is related by structure and meaning to **for** *over* as Latin *sub* is to *super* and Greek ὑπό to ὑπέρ, or as English *on* is to *under*—the one word stands as in a position of comparison with the other.

Gu, gus is the modern form of **co, cos** in the old language representing an older **co(th)**. **Cos** was used before the Article as **gus** now is. **Co** took the form **cu** in combining with the Pronouns and it underwent reduplication; as, **cu-cc-um** = **chugam** *to me*, **cu-c-ut** = **chugat** *to thee.* This shows what the spelling should now be of these compound forms. **Thugam** and **h-ugam** the more common ways of writing are etymologically incorrect, and if the history of the word is to be at all regarded, it must come into composition as **chugam, chucat**, etc. This indeed is as it used to be written.

'**Gu**,' says Stewart, 'was long written with **ch** prefixed; thus, **chugam**, etc. The translators of the Scriptures observing that **ch** neither corresponded to the pronunciation nor made part of the radical preposition exchanged it for **th** and wrote **thugam**, etc. The **th** being no more than a simple aspiration corresponds indeed to the common mode of pronouncing the word. Yet it may be questioned whether **t** even though aspirated ought to have a place if **g** be the only radical Consonant belonging to the Preposition.' This reasoning in the light of present knowledge is insufficient; and the form **h-ugam** which Stewart commends is misleading as may be easily observed. The form superseded by the translators had etymological correctness and historical continuity in its favour, the new and commended forms had all this against them and nothing for them that can be readily appreciated.

There was in old Gaelic another word which had nearly the same forms as **co(th)** but which was of quite different meaning, etymology, and grammatical conduct. The primary form of this word was **con** but it changed to **co** and **cu** and **cos** and by assimilation to **col-** **com-** and **cor-** in certain positions. **Co** on the other hand took the forms **cu** and **cos** in certain positions but it could not properly have an assimilating form—though sometimes we meet with such as **com-mattun**=**gu maduinn** *till morning* where the assimilating **m** would not seem to be necessary. Zeuss treats these words **co** and **con** as one and the same word but there would appear to be good reasons for considering them as two distinct words.

The one **co(th)** means *to, as far as, ad* or *usque ad* and has its kinship with Greek κατά; the other **con** means *with* and has its kinship with Latin *cum* or old Latin *com*.

The one **co(th)** governed the Accusative the other **con** governed the Dative; **co cend**=**gu ceann, o hisul co huasal** =**o iseal gu uasal; conainglib**=*with angels,* **cosnaib gnimaib**= *with the deeds.*

Co(th) combined with the Personal Pronouns in the form **cu—cuccum, cucut, cuci** and **cuicce**=mod. **chugam, chugat,**

chuige and chuice; con did not so combine, its place was taken by le or la *with*—lium, lat, leiss and lae.

Co(th) is even now in full use and still retains its original and historical signification; con is almost entirely lost. The latter is thought to exist in the expressions slat gu leth, mile gu leth *a yard and (with) a half, a mile and (with) a half.*

It is to this, doubtless, that the different government of gus and gu in the modern language is to be traced. Gus governs the Accusative gus a' chlach *to the stone* but gu governs the Dative gu cloich *to a stone.*

Gun is the modern form of older cen and a still older cene. Though ending in a Consonant it causes aspiration; as, gun cheann, gun chas *without head, without foot.* This points to its old Vowel termination. It does not cause aspiration of Dentals; gun nighean, gun duine, gun teine, for reasons already given. It used to govern the Accusative; cen bròn, cen dubha, cen bàs *without grief, sorrow, or death*; and it does so now gun cheann, gun chas.

Iar is not now used in Scottish Gaelic except in connection with the verb, and not even in that position with any regularity. Perhaps it would have been as well to have retained it in such phrases as air sin *after that,* air so *after this* which used to be iarsin, iarso. It was almost entirely limited to the relation of time; as, iar tichte Crist = air teachd do Chriosd *after the coming of Christ,* so that we may venture to look upon such forms as iarnachùl *behind him* as exceptional and irregular. The confusion here arises from the similarity with **ar** which is limited to place or position as **iar** is to time.

It has the same meaning now as it used to have, namely *after*; but it had the secondary meaning of *according to* which it has now altogether lost; **ishe arnathir iar colinn** *he is our father according to the body*. This signification is exactly parallel to that of English in such phrases as *after the flesh.*

Le which used to be frequently written **la**, especially in old Irish Gaelic, does not cause aspiration, and for this reason it is inferred to have had an old form ending in a Consonant, perhaps **leth**, like **coth** which is now **gu**.

Le combined with the Personal Pronouns sometimes as **li**. The First Person has the forms **lim, lium, lem**, the Second **lat**, and the Third **lais, laiss, leiss**, and **less**, and for the Feminine **lae** and **laee**. **Le** took the place of **con** *with* which did not combine with the Pronouns, and of **oc** *at* which only combined with the Third Singular and even with that rarely. The plural forms were **linn, libh,** and **leo**, from which it might be argued that those who write **linn, libh,** and **leo** in the modern language are more correct than those who write **leinn, leibh,** and **leotha**—this last form especially is without excuse.

Mar is not a pure Preposition. It does not appear in the old language, for Zeuss makes no reference to it as a Preposition. The word seems to result from **samail** which is closely kin to Latin *similis* and Greek ὁμαλός. It is also met with as **amhail**, and older **amal** in the *Lebar Brec* **amal larach Lugdach** = **mar larach Lugdaich** *like the house-site of L.* The Welsh has the word in the form **mal** from which it will be seen the transition to or from **mar** is easy. The word is met with in different forms and in various positions as a Conjunction, as an Adverb, as an Adjective, and even as a Noun.

Mr. Macbain points out that the fact of Zeuss not meeting with **mar** in the Glosses is no argument against its antiquity. It is found as Preposition and Adverb as far back as 1100—in the oldest MSS.—and its full form is **immar=ambi+are**, that is the same as **mu** and **ar** *about* and *beside* and therefore *like*.

[marginal note: mu-ar]

It causes aspiration and governs the Dative **mar mhnaoi** *like a woman*; but if the Article intervenes it governs the Accusative **mar a' bhean** *like the woman*.

Mu has suffered a transposition. The old form was **im, imm** and **imb**. It is therefore akin to Latin *ambi* and Greek ἀμφί in history as in meaning. In the combination with Personal Pronouns it remains in its former state untransposed but with **u** for **i**. It is therefore wrong to say, as grammars do, that in the forms **umam umad**, etc., the first syllable is **mu** transposed. The old forms were **imum, imut** and these are indeed often nearer to the more correct modern pronunciation than the forms at present used.

O frequently had the form **ua** in the old language and both forms often took initial **h**—**ho, hua**—**ho belib** *from lips*, **huaitsu** *from you*; but this **h** was not an essential nor perhaps a necessary part of the Preposition

—**othossuch** *from the beginning,* **uambrathrib** *from their brethren.*

The form **ua** was that which combined with the Pronouns in the old language as it is also in the modern **rochuala uaimse**=do chuala (sibh) **uamsa** *which ye heard from me,* **leic uait**=leig uat *let from thee, omit,* **arishuad cach necne**=oir is uaidh gach ecne (eolas) *for from him is every knowledge,* **uadi**=uaithe *from her.*

It is important to note that the Third Person Singular of both genders was in **d, uad** *from him* **uadi** *from her*—plural **uaidib** *from them.* This should enable us to arrive at the correct forms for the modern language, for **uaipe** *from her* **uapa** *from them* as well as **uaithe** *from him* would appear to be wrong. This is referred to in connection with Prepositional Pronouns, p. 140.

Os *above* has now a very limited use. **Oscionn** *above-head, above* is however still in active use; **os bàrr** *above-top, moreover* and **osìseal** *privately* are almost gone out of use; **osàrd** *openly* and **oscàch** *above the rest, pre-eminent* though appearing in dictionaries are perhaps never now used. **Os** took the form **uas** freely and took also initial **h** like **o** *from* **oscach ainmim**=os (cionn) gach ainm *above every name,* **huasgrein** *above the sun,* **ari uasnaflaithib** *O king above the princes.*

This Preposition combined with the Personal Pronoun though now it does not do so. In Patrick's Hymn we find **Crist isum Crist uasum Crist dessum Crist tuathum** *Christ under me—above me—on my right hand—and on my left* i.e. *to right of me—to left.*

Is which was the opposite of **os** is now gone altogether out of use as a separate word. The two forms remain as elements in **iosal** *lowly,* **uasal** *highly, noble,* and in **iochdar** *the bottom,* **uachdar** *the top* or *surface.*

Ri which used to be written **fri** does not cause aspiration though it ends in a Vowel, and for this reason it has been inferred to have formerly ended in a Consonant having perhaps the form **frit** or **vrit**. **Fris** was the form in the old language before the Articles **frisin fer=ris an fhear** *to or against the man.* But the **s** in this position originally belonged to the Article, and the full expression might be written **fri(th)sinfer**. The Welsh form is **gwrth** which through the form **wert** comes near to Latin *vert* which is the nearest and most general meaning of **fri,** namely *ad-vert-us=adversus against.*

Fri is used in one or other of two different senses though the action implied is essentially the same in both cases. It may mean either *motion to* or *motion from* and may be translated *to* in some cases and *from* in others; or as Zeuss expresses it 'ex qua mitescit sensus in significationem motus *ad* aliquem versi vel etiam versi *ab* aliquo; **occath fri diabul=ag cath ri diabhul** *battling against a devil,* **denum maith fricach=deanam maith ri càch** *let me do good to others,* and again **cid torbe doib etarscarad etir friatola et a pecthu=ciod an tairbhe dhoibh eadarsgaradh idir ri an toilean agus ri am peacaidh** *what (is) the profit to them to have at all separated from their desires and from their sins.*

Roimh *before* has old form **ren** which like **in** and **con** and **iarn** dropped **n** and took **s** before the Article or more correctly the **s** of the Article caused the assimilation of the **n** of the Preposition; it is for this reason that the form **coss** is met with. **Resindalm sin=roimh an alm sin** *before that 'alms'—charity*, **isinchruth sin = anns a' chruth sin** *in that form*, **cosalaasa=gus an latha-sa** *to this day*, **iarsindligud=ar reir na dligheachd** *according to custom*.

Ren took the forms **ri** and **re** in certain positions and in composition it was **rem-**. This last was the form combining with the Pronouns and was the immediate predecessor of the **rom-** which combines with the Pronoun in the modern language; **remi** *before her* now **roimpe, remib** *before you* now **roimhibh**. It is not devoid of interest that in some parts of the country the popular pronunciation is nearer to the old spelling than to the modern—if the aspiration is allowed for. It is quite a common thing to hear **ren-a-so** *before this* **re-(mh)-pe** *before her*, **re-(mh)-ibh** *before you*.

Seach of which the older form was **sech** is akin to Latin *sec-us* and Greek ἑκάς. The Welsh is **hep** which gives a good illustration of the change or correspondence of different letters between the two languages that is so interesting to study. Gaelic **s** is Welsh **h** and Gaelic **c** is Welsh **p, seol** *a sail* is **hwyl, sen** *old* is **hen, ceann** *a head* is **pen** and **crann** *a tree* is **pren**.

Seach has various shades of meaning all diverging from the primary idea of going by, past, or beyond something. It was found by Zeuss joined to the Personal Pronoun only in one instance **seccu** *past them*. It does not combine in the modern language if the Adverb **seachad** *past* does not come by this way, and this is suggested by such similar formations as **fodha, trid, roimhe, tarsuinn** etc. which are all Adverbs of the form of the Prepositional Pronoun. It governs the Accusative; **seach a' chlach** *past the stone*.

Tar is directly related to Latin *trans*. It had a form **tars** with the Article in the old language. It does not cause aspiration. It is the only one of the Prepositions that takes the Genitive Case; **chaidh e thar an eich** *he went over the horse*, **chaidh iad thar na beinne** *they went over the mountain*, **thainig mi thar na h-aimhne** *I came across the river*.

The fact that **tar** governs the Genitive arouses suspicion that it is a Noun, but this is not apparent though it must be observed that like a Noun it aspirates a Genitive Plural **thar bheann** *over* or *across mountains*. It will do no harm in any case to associate it in memory with that considerable class of Nouns which in certain positions must be esteemed Prepositions—that is, when a proper Preposition is not expressed before them; **chaidh an ceol feadh na fidhle** *the music has gone throughout the fiddle*=every one has heard about the matter, it is no secret; **bha e cul an tighe** *he was (at the) back of the house*, **ceart mar a ta na beannta tric timchioll Ierusaleim** *just as are the mountains frequent around* (a Noun) *Jerusalem*.

Troimh had old form **tri** and **tre**, and **tris** with the Article; **trisnasen pecthu**=**tre na seann pheacaidh** *through the old sins*. It caused aspiration as it does now, even in the old language; hence it is inferred to have originally ended in a Vowel. So the modern form may be looked upon as so far incorrect coming most likely by false analogy with **roimh** *before*, which has been shown to have originally ended in a Consonant. **Tri** is met with in very old Gaelic; and the forms in kindred languages point towards the same thing—to show that **troimh** always ended in a Vowel. **Troi** or **trwi** for **tre** was the form in old Welsh; in modern

Welsh it is **trwy** which is exactly the same as **troimh** of modern Gaelic.

Troimh used to combine with the Pronouns as **tri** and **tre**; **trium, triut, triit,** and **trée,** but this combination is now fallen out of use except perhaps the Third Person Singular of the Masculine **trid** and the more commonly used Emphatic form **tridsan.** This form **trid** is itself used as a Preposition; **trid ghlinn dorcha sgàil a' bhàis** *through the dark valley of the shadow of (the) death,* but it seems better to refer this construction to the usage stated under **tar**—for **trid** also governs the Genitive.

The Preposition **fiad** *coram* of the old language is gone quite out of use without leaving a trace behind, if it be not in the word **fianuis** *a witness,* which has been thought to be **fiadh-ghnuis** *before the presence of.* The Syntax as well as the feeling in such expressions as **am fianuis righrean agus thuatha** *in the presence of kings and peoples* is certainly very close to **fiad rigu ocus tuatha** the old form, in which **fiad** is the pure Preposition. Etymology however would seem to contradict this (see Macbain's Dictionary).

Ol also is lost, if it is not the root in **a nall** and **thall**=a-n-all, to-all. It had various meanings, *super, de, propter* etc. though its use was not very extensive.

Iar is preserved pure in composition in such words as **iar-mad** *a remnant,* **iar-ogha** *a great grandson;* and **ri** is preserved in its old form **frith** in **frith-rathad** *a bye-way,* **frith-bhac** *the barb of a hook,* **frith-ainm** *a nickname.*

PREPOSITIONS

The Prepositions combine with the Personal Pronouns to form the PREPOSITIONAL PRONOUNS as follows:—

	SINGULAR 1	2	3 MASC.	3 FEM.	PLURAL 1	2	3
	mi *me*	tu *thou*	e *him*	i *her*	sinn *us*	sibh *you*	iad *them*
aig *at*	agam	agad	aige	aice	againn	agaibh	aca
air *on*	orm	ort	air	oirre	oirnn	oirbh	orra
ann *in*	annam	annad	ann	innte	annainn	annaibh	annta
as *out of*	asam	asad	as	aiste	asainn	asaibh	asta
de *of*	diom	diot	deth	dith	dinn	dibh	diubh
do *to*	domh	dut	dà	di	duinn	duibh	doibh
eadar *between*					eadarainn	eadaraibh	eatorra
fo *under*	fodham	fodhad	fodha	foipe	fodhainn	fodhaibh	fopa
gu *towards*	chugam	chugad	chuige	chuice	chugainn	chugaibh	chuca
le *with*	leam	leat	leis	leithe	leinn	leibh	leo
mu *about*	umam	umad	uime	uimpe	umainn	umaibh	umpa
ua *from*	uam	uat	uaidh	uaithe	uainn	uaibh	uapa
ri *to*	rium	riut	ris	rithe	rinn	ribh	riu
romh *before*	romham	romhad	roimhe	roimpe	romhainn	romhaibh	rompa
thar *over*	tharam	tharad	thairis air	thairis oirre	tharainn	tharaibh	tharta
tromh *through*	tromham	tromhad	troimhe	troimpe	tromhainn	tromhaibh	trompa

All Prepositional Pronouns may take an Emphatic form; **agam-sa, agad-sa, da-san; duinne** (for **duinn-ne**), **umaibh-se, tharta-san.**

The Third Plural is the same for both Genders.

It will be observed that **eadar** *between* cannot have a Singular here.

It is usually stated that the elements here shown—the Preposition and the Pronouns—are the constituents more or less changed of the Compound forms. To a certain extent this is correct. The Pronominal element is comparatively clear in the First and Second Persons of the Singular and Plural but in the Third Persons it is by no means always clear. The explanation sometimes given that the terminal Vowel of the Third Plural has resulted from the aspiration of **iad** is quite untenable.

The forms of the Third Person Singular present a few points of interest:

It is usually said that the Pronoun element has disappeared altogether in **air, ann, as, leis, ris** and that the Preposition alone remains. It is not quite so. When in the old language a Preposition governed the Dative it sometimes took a form in **d** for the Masculine of the Pronoun, which **d** itself was perhaps the remnant of a still older and fuller form. **Indid** *in him* and **uad** *from him* had this form. The last **n** of **ann** therefore represents this older **d** as we find it frequently does, **clann** for **cland**.

On the other hand when a Preposition governed the Accusative, the form was in **s, les** *with him,* **fris** *to him,* **tarais** *over him,* and once in **t, trit** *through him.* The forms in **s** and **t** still remain in **leis, ris** and **trid. Tarais** has lost its full meaning; but is like some others of the Prepositional Pronouns used in an adverbial sense; **seachad, fodha,** etc. The Preposition **as** though it governed the Dative took the form in **s—ni beram ass** (*non feremus ex eo*).

The Third Singular Masculine **air** is peculiar in being the only one of its kind which has **a** in its form. It is to be remembered that **for** is the Preposition entering into this combination, hence the **o** form throughout **(f)orm, (f)ort,** etc. **Foir** was the old Third Singular Masculine and **fuiri** the Feminine. There is room therefore to suspect that the Preposition **ar** came into contact at this point (see **ar**). The old form in combination with **ar** was **airi** *against him* and the **i** may have dropped or been thrown forward into the body of the word as in **mori=muir.**

The **a** of **dà** and **fodha** arises no doubt through the influence of the broad **o** on the termination. The old forms were **dò** and **foi**. The forms in **e—aige, chuige, uime, roimhe** and **troimhe** had older forms **oca** or **occa, cuci** or **cucci, immbi, trid** (masc.) and **tree** (fem.).

There does not seem to be any reason for writing **deth.** The old form was **de** which is correct in structure and consonant with the modern pronunciation. The same is true of **dith** *of her* also. It is almost certain that **th** which serves no purpose was introduced without any reference to the history or the phonetics of the language.

The Feminine forms are extremely important.

If we compare the pronunciation of these with that of the Masculine forms it will be at once noticed that there is a peculiarly heavy *asperation* on the second syllable always. For this there must be some cause—some constant cause, and common to all the Feminine combinations.

The form **innte** is interesting for various reasons. It is the only one of the **ann** combinations which has retained the earlier form of the Preposition **in**. We know that the old Feminine form was **inndi**, and that now it is **innte**. We have seen that **d** before aspirated **s** hardens in the later and modern language to **t**. Therefore we venture to infer that the form **innte** may be resolved into **ind-she**, the **s** not pronounced, being aspirated. From this we should derive a form **se** for the Feminine Pronominal element which in its aspirated form comes into combination with all the Prepositions and hardens the preceding Consonant. This is the key to all the Feminine forms.

```
ag-she     = aice (g hardened to c)
as-she     = aiste (t for the second s phonetic)
(f)or-she  = oirre (r for the aspirated s)
ind-she    = innte (d hardened to t)
fo-she     = foithe (sh to th)
cu-c-she   = chuice (c hardened or aspirated)
le(th)-she = leithe (sh to th)
imb-she    = uimpe (b hardened to p)
ua-she     = uaithe (sh to th)
ri(th)-she = rithe (sh to th)
rem-she    = roimpe (m to p)
trem-she   = troimpe (m to p)
```

It will be observed that in all these forms the small sound of **se** determines by retrogressive assimilation the introduction of **i** in the first syllable when the vowel of the Preposition is Broad.

While the **p** in **uimpe**, **roimpe** and **troimpe** is a phonetic necessity, that in **foipe** and **uaipe** of the modern language is phonetically and historically wrong. Irish Gaelic preserves the correct forms **fuithe** and **uaithe**. The wrong forms of Scottish Gaelic doubtless have arisen from a false analogy with **uimpe, roimpe, troimpe** but they have no excuse either of elegance or convenience for their retention. The form **uaithe** used for the Masculine is grossly incorrect. With regard to the history of the word it does not follow the ordinary laws of change. The old form was **uad** which would be represented now by **uadh** or **uaidh** and which would be more consonant with modern pronunciation than **uaithe**. The correct form **uadh** is retained in Irish. The form **uaithe** is Feminine in structure, analogous to **leithe** and **rithe**; it is correctly used for the Feminine in Irish.

All the forms of the Third Plural have the Accusative termination except **doibh** and **diubh**. These two have the Dative termination. The old Accusative was in **iu** or **u**; so, **riu** is now the only pure Accusative form remaining.

The Third Plural incorporates a form **siu** as the Third Singular Feminine does **se** and with a similar effect, as may be seen, on the Consonants of the Preposition. The final **a** may therefore be taken to represent old **u**, and indeed it may be observed that **û** is nearer the modern pronunciation than **a** is.

The old forms for the Second and Third Persons with **do** and **di** were **diib** *from you* and **diib** *from* or *of them*; **diib** *to you* and **doib** *to them*.

Fopa, and **uapa** of the Third Plural are wrong for the same reason as **foipe** and **uaipe** have been shown to be. The Irish retains **futha** and **uatha** which are correct.

Leotha is also so far wrong for **th** is not necessary. The old form was **leo** as it is in modern Irish also.

Tharta or **tharsta** is for **tars-siu** and that explains the **t**. It is the same as in **aiste** for **as-she**—the second **s** hardening phonetically.

COMPOUND PREPOSITIONS are formed by the association or union of a Preposition and a Noun. From the point of view of Gaelic grammar exclusively this class might conveniently be dispensed with. It may however be helpful to the learner to study the following list and the observations made regarding it.

a bhàrr *from, down from*

a chum *for the purpose of*

a dh' easbhuidh *in want of*

a dh' fhios *to the knowledge of*

a dh' ionnsaidh *towards*

a dhìth *for want of, without*

a los *in order to, with the intention of*

a reir *according to*

a thaobh *regarding, respecting*

am bun *waiting on, near to*

am fianuis *in the presence of*

am fochair *in presence*

air bheulthaobh *in front of, before*

air chulthaobh *at back of, behind*

air cheann *against the time of*

air fad *throughout*

air feadh *among, through*

air ghaol *for the love of*

air ghràdh *for the love of*

air muin *on the back of, mounted on*

air sgàth *for the sake of*

air son *on account of, for*

air tòir *in pursuit of*

comhla ri *along with, together with* .

PREPOSITIONS

am measg *amidst, among*

an aghaidh *against*

an aite *instead of, in place of*

an ceann *in the end, at the expiration of*

an coinneamh *to meet*

an cois *at foot, hard by, near to*

an comhail *to meet*

an dàil *searching for, in the track of*

an éiric *in return for, in ransom for*

an lathair *in presence of*

an lorg *in track of, in consequence of*

an taice *in support of, in contact*

as leth *in behalf of*

as eugmhais *without*

gu ruig *until, as far as*

fa chomhair *before, opposite*

fa chùis *by reason of, because*

faisg air *near to*

lamh ri *at hand, near to*

maille ri *along with*

mu choinneamh *opposite, before*

mu dheibhinn *respecting*

mu thimchioll *about, regarding*

mu thuaiream *about (estimate)*

mu'n cuairt *around*

o bhàrr *from the top, off*

os ceann *above, overhead*

tar éis *post, pro*

trid *through, by means of*

os cionn *above*

It is not unlikely that **air** in most of these phrases should be **ar** and that it should perhaps always aspirate; **ar bheulthaobh, ar chulthaobh, ar fhad, ar fheadh**—the same as **ar cheann, ar ghaol, ar ghràdh**.

These Compound Prepositions may be divided into two classes:—

1. A large class in which the Preposition is first; **am measg, an aghaidh.**

2. A small class in which the Preposition is last; **maille ri, faisg air.**

In almost all of the first class the Preposition and the Noun may be separated and the Possessive Pronouns may be introduced between them; thus, **air mo shon** *for my sake,* **fa do chomhair** *before thy presence,* **os an cionn** *above them.*

The following do not admit this construction, namely, **a bharr, a chum, a los, mu'n cuairt, gu ruig, an ceann.**

In those of the second class a Personal Pronoun may combine with the Preposition after the manner of Prepositional Pronouns; **maille ri-um** *together with me,* **lamh ri-ut** *beside thee.*

After **air, as** and **os** the Possessive is written entire before a Consonant; **air do chulthaobh** *at back of you = behind you,* **as mo leth** *in my behalf,* **os bhur cionn** *above you.*

But before a Vowel-initial, or f-aspirated, the Vowel of the Possessive is dropped; **air m' aghaidh** *on my front = forward,* **as m' eugmhais** *without me,* **air fheadh** *throughout him.* The harder **a** of the Feminine however remains and usually takes **h** '*in hiatu*'; **as a h-eugmhais** *without her,* **air a feadh** *throughout her.* It is well to indicate the elision of the Masculine Pronoun before Vowels; thus, **as 'eugmhais,** but with initial **f** the aspiration serves this purpose—**air fheadh** and it is not necessary to indicate the elision.

Between two vowels **mo** and **do** drop the **o**; **do m' ionnsaidh** *towards me,* **a m' easbhuidh** *in want of me = without me.* But the Masculine **a** is not dropped in this position, it is the Vowel of the Preposition that is dropped; thus, **d' a ionnsaidh** *towards him.*

The Preposition **a** for **do** is only used in the First and Second Person Singular; **a m' reir** *according to me,* but **d' a chois, d' a cois** *to his, to her—foot.* So in the Plural **do ar cois, do bhur cois, do an cois,** *to our—your—their foot.*

After **an**, of which **am** is but the form before labials, **mo** and **do** are reversed and become **am, ad**; thus, **ann am cheann** *in my head*, **ann ad chorp** *in thy body* which forms are usually contracted into '**nam cheann**, '**nad chorp**—especially in the spoken language.

When the reversed Pronoun is introduced between labials thus **am am mheasg, am ad mheasg** a difficulty arises which has led to a good deal of confusion in writing. The full forms are intolerable to the spoken speech and they are therefore contracted into **am mheasg ad mheasg** which have been variously written '**am mheasg, am' mheasg, a' 'm mheasg, a' m' mheasg** according to the fancy of the writer. The form '**am mheasg** implies that the whole Preposition is fallen out and that this **am** is the inverted Pronoun alone. **Am' mheasg** would suggest that the Pronoun is dropped, the **am** being the Preposition. **A' 'm mheasg** indicates that **m** of the Preposition and **a** of the Pronoun is dropped, and **a' m'** that **m** of the Preposition and **o** of the Possessive have fallen out.

Regarding the last form **a' m'** it takes no account of the transposition of the Pronoun in this position; and being therefore wrong its other disadvantages need not be discussed.

The first and second forms '**am** and **am'** are either both right or both wrong. If the suggestion is to be admitted that the whole Preposition or the whole Pronoun may drop out, the one form is as good as the other. But as neither the Preposition nor the Pronoun can altogether fall out either as regards its meaning or grammatical influence both these forms are wrong.

The third form **a' 'm** is correct but clumsy and troublesome. There does not seem to be any good reason why **am** simply might not be written as it is spoken. It cannot cause any confusion or difficulty. It cannot be mistaken for the Preposition or it would not cause aspiration nor for the Pronoun alone or it would not be reversed.

K

This combination used to be written **im** and **am** without causing any confusion.

Am measg can only be rightly used in the Plural, or in the Singular with Collective Nouns. **'N ar measg** *in our midst*, **am measg nan craobh** *among the trees*, **am measg na mine** *amongst the meal*.

The **n** in **mu 'n cuairt** is interesting. It does not belong to the Preposition **mu**, and it was not in the old forms *e.g.* **imum imacuairt**=**umam mu 'n cuairt** *round about me*. Some have thought it is the Article which has got into this peculiar phrase; but it seems rather to be an **n** that has slipped in to satisfy a phonetic felt want before **c**, according to the principle stated p. 18.

Mr. Macbain maintains that this **n** is the Article and that the expression means 'about the circuit' (of). Stokes, in what seems to be a parallel example **immuaneclis** *around the church* says the Article is affixed not to the Preposition **imm** but to the Compound Preposition **immu**.

Tareis is an old form not now used. It belonged to the same class as **tarcenn** (pro) **archenn** or **archiunn** (coram) **do reir**=**a reir**, **indead**=**an deigh**, **do chum**=**a chum**.

Gu ruig does not govern the Genitive like the others but the Accusative; **gu ruig an tigh** *as far as the house*. The old form in Irish was **con-icc-i** and **corrici**. In the *Book of Deer* it is **gonic**, and this is even yet frequently heard in conversation.

CHAPTER IX—OF CONJUNCTIONS

CONJUNCTIONS are used to connect words and clauses in a sentence; as, **chunnaic mi Domhnull agus Tòmas ach cha'n fhaca mi thusa** *I saw Donald and Thomas but I did not see you.*

The following are the Simple Conjunctions—

ach *but*	**mun** *before, lest*
agus *and*	**mur** *if not*
an, am *whether*	**na** *than*
co *as*	**nach** *that not*
ged *though*	**na'n** *if*
gu *that, so that*	**no** *or*
ma *if*	**o** *since*
mar *like as*	**oir** *for*

Most of these have been already referred to as 'Particles.'

Ach like English *but* has several kindred significations; **cha charaid ach caraid na h-airce** *he is no friend unless he is the friend of (my) need,* **cha bu ruith ach leum** *not only run but rather jump*—at it, **cha d' rinn mi ach sgur** *I have but just stopped or ceased.*

Agus is the pure copulative, but it has other uses also; **nach truagh leat mi 's mi 'm priosan** *do you not pity me and I in prison,* **cho luath agus is urrainn domh** *as quickly* or *swiftly as I can,* **am bi thu cho maith agus mo fhreagairt** *will you be so good as to answer me.*

An is evidently the same form as the interrogative **an**; **saoil an tig e** *think you whether he will come,* **feoraich an eirich iad** *ask if* or *whether they will rise.*

Co though usually classed as a Conjunction, does not appear to be so used in the modern language. In such expressions as **cho mòr** *as* or *so great* **cho** seems to have come directly from the old Preposition **con** *with.* **Gu** *until* on the other hand is for old **co(th)** as in **gu ruig an tigh**=co ro-icc *as far as* the house lit. **co** *to* or *till,* **ro** particle of past time, and **icc** *to come*; therefore *till shall have come*—the house; **Calum beag a chur a dhìth gu Murchadh mòr a reamhrachadh** *putting little C. to death in order to fatten big Murdoch.*

Mun is frequently heard as **mus** among purely native

speakers. It used to be **mos** in Old Irish—a verbal Particle of adverbial force; **mosricab mo mochlige** *I shall soon* (**mos**) *reach my early grave* (**lige**). Its simplest use is seen in **fada mun tig an latha** *long ere the day comes*. It means *lest* in **fluich do shiul mun gabh i air** *wet your eye lest it affect him* (lit. *take* or *catch on him*); and it has a very peculiar use in for instance **mun d' thubhairt iad** *as they say*.

Na is for old **inda**, usually along with **as**; as **laigu deacht maicc inda as deacht athar** *the godhood of a son is less than that of a father* 'as say the heretics,' **bu mou he indas cech cuibrend** Mod. **bu mhò e na gach cuibhrionn** *he was greater than all portions* or *gifts* **bahairde he indat tige in baile** *he was higher than the houses of the town*. These are very important for they explain the forms used in Comparison.

Nach has a very peculiar usage in **mur tig an righ nach fhuirich e** *if the king won't come, well let him stay where he is* or *will he not stay*. The double use of **nach** as Relative and Interrogative already given, explains this peculiarity of expression.

No is frequently written **na**; **thusa na mise** *you or I*. It is used like English *or* as a simple 'disjunctive' **fear nach treig a chailleag no a chompanach** *a man that will not forsake his girl or his comrade*, and for *otherwise* **dean greim no tuitidh tu** *keep hold or (otherwise) you will fall*, but **neo** is more commonly used in this latter sense.

Oir seems to have come from the aspirating Preposition **ar** which form it has in the old language, **arissed isuaisliu** = **oir is e is uaisle** *because it is this that is noblest*.

A number of phrases are usually classed as COMPOUND CONJUNCTIONS — because they represent the Conjunctions of English; **a chionn gu** *to the end that, because,* **air an aobhar sin** *on that account, therefore,* **gun fhios nach** *perhaps,* **uime sin** *therefore.*

CHAPTER X—OF INTERJECTIONS

INTERJECTIONS are sounds, words, or phrases expressive of some sudden emotion or intense feeling. They are numerous in Gaelic, but as they are for the most part provincial and arbitrary, only a few of the better known are here given with their signification.

a! *various shades of meaning, pity, wonder, etc.*
ach *nasty, repulsive*
obh, obh *sad, sorrowful*
oit *hot*

och, och *heartsore*
oich *sore, from sudden pain*
ud, ud *no, no—it can't be*
cuist, uist *(you) don't say so!*
fuich *nasty, offensive*

mo chràdh *my torment*
mo chreach *my plundering*
mo dhòruinn *my anguish*
mo laochan *my hero, well-done*
mo mhasladh *my disgrace*
mo nàire *my shame*
mo naire's mo leaghadh lit. *my shame and my melting.*
mo thruaighe *my misery*

These Possessive Phrases mean that what has just happened or come to knowledge is to the speaker *a torment—a disgrace* etc.; but **mo mhasladh** and the phrases following may be addressed to a second person, *shame on you—I pity you*, etc.

PART III—OF DERIVATION AND COMPOSITION

CHAPTER I—OF DERIVATION

THE parts of speech formed by derivation from other words are Nouns, Adjectives, and Verbs. These are derived chiefly from Nouns and Adjectives, and a few from Verbs.

DERIVATIVE NOUNS may be classed as follows.

1. Abstract Nouns in **as, achd**, are formed from Adjectives and from Nouns; thus, **ceartas** *justice* from **ceart** *just*, **càirdeas** *friendship* from **caraid** *a friend*, and **naomhachd** *holiness* from **naomh** *holy*, **goibhneachd** *smithwork* or *the trade of smith* from **gobhain** *a smith*.

2. Abstract Nouns in **e** from the Genitive Feminine of Adjectives, and in **ad** from the Third Comparative; **doille** *blindness* from **dall** *blind*, **uaisle** *nobility* from **uasal** *noble*; and **doillead** *blindness*, **uaislead** *nobleness*, which forms are used to express a degree of the quality implied *e.g.* **air 'uaislead** *however noble he be*, **air a h-uaislead** *however noble she be*.

3. Nouns in **air, iche,** and **seach** signifying persons or agents are derived from other Nouns; **piobair** *a piper* from **piob** *a pipe*, **cealgair** *a deceiver* from **cealg** *deceit*;

DERIVATION

marcaiche *a rider* or *horseman* from Old **marc** *a horse*, **sgeulaiche** *a reciter of tales, a novelist* from **sgeul** *a tale*; and **oinseach** *a foolish woman*, from Old **on** *foolish*.

4. Diminutives in **an** and in **ag**—formed from Nouns and from Adjectives; **lochan** *a small lake* from **loch** *a lake*, **bradag** *a thievish girl* from **braid** *theft*, so **ciaran** *the dusky* (*one*) from **ciar** *dark-grey*.

These Diminutives are often formed from the Genitive of their Primitives; as, **feur** *grass* gen. **feoir**—**feoirnean** *a blade of grass*, **moll** *chaff* gen. **muill**—**muillein** *a particle of chaff*.

5. Collective Nouns in **ridh** and **lach** formed from Nouns; **macruidh** (*a band of*) *sons or young men*, **oigridh** *young people*, **teaghlach** *a family*.

6. Nouns in **ach** chiefly Patronymics are formed from Proper Names; **Domhnullach** from **Domhnull** *Donald, one of the Macdonalds*, **Camshronach** *one of the Camerons*.

Collective Nouns in **ach** are formed from Nouns; as, **giubhsach** *a firwood* from **giubhas** *fir*, **iubhrach** *a yew copse* from **iubhar** *yew*.

DERIVATIVE ADJECTIVES in **ach**, **ail**, and **mhor** or **or** are all derived from Nouns; as, **sunntach** *cheerful* from **sunnt** *glee* or *cheer*, **firinneach** *truthful* from **firinn** *truth*; **fearail** *manly* from **fear** *a man*, **càirdeal** *friendly* from **caraid** *a friend*; **neartmhor** *powerful* from **neart** *strength*, **ceolmhor** *melodious* from **ceol** *music*.

DERIVATIVE VERBS, formed from Nouns and Adjectives, have termination **ich** and are mostly Transitive; **gealaich** *whiten* from **geal** *white*, **cuimhnich** *remember* from **cuimhne** *memory*.

CHAPTER II—OF COMPOSITION

ALL Compound words consist of two parts, exclusive of the derivative terminations just referred to. The word denoting the accessory idea is prefixed to that denoting the principal idea.

The combination of Noun with Noun and with Adjective, of Adjective with Noun, and of Adjective with Adjective, as well as the changes on the initial Consonant of the second term has been already referred to, p. 61.

A Verb may combine with a Noun, with an Adjective, or with a Preposition to form a Compound Verb; as, **cùl-shleamhnuich** *backslide*, **geur-lean** *persecute*, **eadar-mhìnich** *interpret*.

The following are the prefixes most commonly used in Composition: Prefixes which mean *not* or make the contrary of the words to which they are attached; as, **an, ana, as** and **eas, di, mi, neo**.

An passes into **am** before Labials, **amh** before aspirates and liquids, **ain** also and **aim, aimh** for correspondence, and **eu** before *Tenues*—changing to ao and ea.

An, ana, and **ain** signifies *faulty excess*, **ath** *again*, **bith** *ever*, **co** *together* ∴ *equally* or *mutually*, **fìor** *very*,

im and **iom** *around* or *about,* **ion** *worthy* or *fit,* **sior** *ever,* and **so** denoting *good quality* and **do** *bad.*

Co has other forms **con, coin, com, comh, coimh** and **coi** according to the following forms and sounds :

From these are formed

an-shocair *unrest*	**ao-trom** *not heavy* ∴ *light*
amadan *a fool*	**ea-slan** *not whole* ∴ *diseased*
amh-arus *distrust*	**ana-ceartas** *injustice*
ain-eolas *ignorance*	**as-creidimh** *ex-faith* ∴ *heresy*
aim-beairt *misdeed*	**eas-caraid** *ex-friend* ∴ *enemy*
aimh-leathan *not broad* ∴ *narrow*	**di-meas** *depreciation*
eu-dòchas *despair*	**mi-chothrom** *unfairness*
	neo-ghlan *unclean*

So also

an-dàna *over-bold*	**coimh-cheangal** *covenant*
ain-neart *oppression, over-force*	**coin-neamh** *a meeting*
ana-cruas *over-severity, cruelty*	**com-panach** *a companion*
ath-fhàs *new* or *re-growth*	**comh-chord** *concord, agree*
bith-bhuan *ever-lasting*	**mi-chlis** *awkward*
co-chomunn *communion*	**iom-ghaoth** *a whirlwind*
con-altradh *conversation*	**ion-mholta** *praiseworthy*
coi-meas *comparison*	**do-char** *a hurt,* **so-char** *a benefit*

Amadan=**am**+**met** for **ment** the same as Lat. *ment* and Eng. *mind* ∴ *the mind-less one* ; **amharus**=**am**+**iress** old word for *faith* ∴ *faithless.*

Coinneamh=**con**+**neamh** root **nes** *to come* ∴ *to come together* ; **companach**=Lat. **com-pani-ô**='*co-bread-man*' ; **conaltradh**= **con-alt-radh** ?—**alt** *a joint.*

Other elements and the earlier stages of Composition are fully treated in Mr. Macbain's Dictionary.

PART IV—OF SYNTAX

CHAPTER I—OF THE SENTENCE

SYNTAX treats of the relation and order of Words in a Sentence.

A SIMPLE SENTENCE consists of three or of two essential parts—Predicate, Subject, and Object if the Verb is Transitive, or Predicate and Subject if the Verb is Intransitive; **mharbh sealgair damh** *a hunter killed a stag*, **thuit craobh** *a tree fell*.

The simplest sentence is one in which each of the Parts is a single word, but each Part may have an enlargement or addition of one or more Words or Phrases.

1. **Mosglamaid** gu suilbhir ait *let us awaken cheerfully, gladly*.

2. **Dh'imich an Garbh** mòr mac Stairn (*the*) *Garv the great son of Starno went forth*.

3. **Chunnaic an Garbh** treun-fheara iomraiteach Fhinn *the G. saw the brave renowned warriors of Fionn*.

The Gaelic words in ordinary type are Enlargements or logical Limitations of the essential Parts (1) of the Predicate; (2) of the Subject; (3) of the Object.

The Order of a Prose Sentence is always—first, the Predicating Verb—next, the Subject with its Enlargements—then, the Object with its Enlargements—and lastly, the Enlargements of the Predicate; **Labhair**—

an duin' eireachdail—mu ar monaidhean farsuinn—gu socrach reidh *the noble man spoke about our wide mountain-ranges—easily and fluently.*

A COMPOUND SENTENCE consists of two or more Simple and Independent Sentences; **duisg suas a Ghaidhlig, tog do ghuth, na biodh ort geilt no sgàth** *Awake Gaelic, raise your voice, fear not.*

Ghineadh iad, 'us rugadh iad, 'us thogadh iad, 'us dh' fhàs, Chaidh stràc de'n t-saoghal thairis orr', 'S ma dheireadh—fhuair iad bàs.—*Rob Donn.*

A COMPLEX SENTENCE consists of one Principal Simple Sentence and one or more Dependent Sentences.

The members of Compound and Complex Sentences are called Clauses.

A Dependent or Subordinate Clause may take the place of a Noun, Adjective, or Adverb in relation to the Parts of the Principal Clause.

Innis (Prin. Cl.)—c' aite 'n robh do thriall (Noun Cl.)—nuair bha na siantan fionnar (Adv. Cl.) *tell—where thy travel was—while the elements were cold*; nach nàrach e (Noun Cl.)—**ars mise** (Prin. Cl.) *is not he bashful said I*; **so, ars esan, Deoch-slainte**—nach diult sibh (Adj. Cl.)—**Tir nam Beann nan Gleann 's nan Gaisgeach** *here said he is a Toast—which you will not refuse—The Land of Bens and Glens and Heroes*; **sean aois—a chromas an t-ard** (Adj. Cl.) *old age which bends down the lofty.*

Mar cheathach tra-noin air an t-sliabh	(Adv. Ph.)
Triallaidh an deo ag imeachd uainn	(Prin. Cl.)
Far nach teirig grian no gràdh,	(Adv. Cl.)
Far am maireann àdh nan sonn.	(Adv. Cl.)

A Phrase—without a finite Verb—may take the position of Adjective or of Adverb.

Cairibh mi—ri taobh nan allt (Adv. Phrase)—**a shiubhlas mall le ceumaibh ciuin** (Adj. Cl.) *lay me by the side of the streams—that journey slowly with gentle steps*; **tha am fearann ag eiridh—gu corrach cas** (Adv. Ph.)—**air an laimh dheis** (Adv. Ph.) *the land rises abruptly on the right hand*; **bha Suaineart—le a chnocan** (Adj. Ph.)—**'s le a thulaichean boidheach** (Adj. Ph.)—**a' deanamh gairdeachais ann am blàs an fheasgair shamhruidh** (Adj. Ph.) *S. with its hills and pretty knolls was rejoicing in the warmth of the summer evening.*

CHAPTER II—OF CONCORD

UNDER Concord is to be considered the Agreement of the Article with its Noun, of the Adjective with its Noun, of a Pronoun with its Antecedent, of a Verb with its Nominative, and of one Noun with another.

AGREEMENT OF THE ARTICLE AND NOUN

The Article agrees with its Noun in Gender, Number, and Case.

FORM.—It agrees in form with the word following, whether Noun, Adjective or Qualifying word. The essential form of the Article depends on Declension, but it is also determined by the Phonetic relation of the words next before or after it. This has been already considered at some length. The form of the Noun also has been considered (pp. 23, 24).

ORDER.—(1) The Article is always placed before its Noun, and next to it, except when an Adjective intervenes; **an duine** *the man.*

If an Adjective simple or qualified precedes the Noun the Article is placed before the Adjective or before the Qualifying word; **an droch dhuine** *the bad man,* **am fior dhroch dhuine** *the very bad man.*

(2) An Ordinal Numeral always takes the Article before it; as, **an treas là** *the third day.* A Cardinal Numeral may or may not take it—according as the Noun to which the Numeral refers is, or is not, used definitely; **an aon fhear** *the one man,* **aon fhear** *one man*; **na tri fir** *the three men,* **tri fir** *three men.*

The Cardinal forms **a h-aon, a dha,** etc., take the grammatical place of Nouns; **fhuair mi a dha** *I found two.* This form never has a Noun expressed and not even understood, but there is a reference implied to a Noun or subject which must have preceded in the conversation.

(3) When one Noun governs another the governing Noun does not take the Article, even though its signification is limited; **ceann an tighe** *the end of the house,* **toiseach na h-oibre** *the beginning of the work.* And if the governed Noun has a Possessive before it, neither Noun has the Article **guth mo ghraidh** *the voice of my love.*

(4) The Article is necessary before a Noun in the following instances:

(a) When the noun is the object of an interrogation; **co am fear** *who (is) the man?* **ciod an tairbhe** *what (is) the profit?*

(b) When it is followed by the Demonstratives **so, sin, sud** or **ud**; **am fear so** *this man*=*the man here*, **an tigh ud** *yon house.*

(c) When it follows the Verb **is** with an Adjective; **is maith an gnothach sin** *that is good business*, **bu ghlan na gillean iad** *they were handsome lads.*

(d) When it is the name of a virtue, a vice, a disease, a metal, or denotes a species; **an fhìrinn** *the truth* ἡ ἀλήθεια, **a' bhreac** *the smallpox*, **an t-òr** *gold or the gold*, **mac an duine** *the son of man(kind).*

(e) When it is the name of a country; **An Fhraing** *France* la France, **A' Ghreig** *Greece*. Except **Sasunn** *England* and **Alba** *Scotland* **Eirinn** *Ireland*—but the latter two sometimes take it in the Genitive; **eachdruidh na h-Alba** *the history of Scotland*, **fearann na h-Eireann** *the land of Ireland.*

(f) When it is a Patronymic; **an Siosalach** *the Chisholm*, **na Domhnullaich** *the Macdonalds.*

(g) When a Personal Name is marked out for distinction; **thuirt an t-Oscar** *(the) Oscar said*, **dàn an Deirg** *the lay of Dargo.*

(h) When possession of a definite object is expressed by the idiom in **aig**; **is e so an t-each agamsa** *this is my horse.*

(5) With Nouns in Apposition—when a proper name is followed by a Noun indicating the trade or profession or calling of the person named, the Article is used before the second Noun:

(a) If it is a compound Noun; **Alasdair an ceardumha** *Alexander the copper-smith.*

(b) If the Proper Name is more than one word; **Ian Caimbeul am maor** *John Campbell the sheriff-officer.*

(c) If the Name is followed by more than one Adjective; **Mòrag bheag bhoidheach a' bhanarach** *pretty little Sarah the milkmaid.*

But the Article is not used at all, if the Name and the Noun in apposition are each Masculine and a single word; as, **Dughall taillear** *Dugald (the) tailor*—or if there is only one Adjective **Eobhan ban ciobair** *fair Evan the shepherd.* Though a Feminine Noun does not have it expressed the construction shows that it is implied; as, **Ceit 'bhanarach** *Kate the milkmaid* in which the Noun is aspirated though the Article is not written, nor spoken.

Agreement of the Adjective and Noun

An Adjective agrees with its Noun in Gender, Number, and Case.

Form.—When an Adjective refers to more than one Noun of different Genders, it agrees with the Noun nearest to it; **lair agus each maith** *a good mare and a* *good horse,* **each agus lair mhaith** *a good horse and a good mare.*

Some Collective Nouns, as **clann, muinntir, oigridh,** etc., take the Plural of the Adjective in the Nominative Singular, but in the other cases the Adjective agrees; **clann bheaga** *little children,* **muinntir òga** *young people;* but **cleas na cloinne bige** *the manner of the little children.*

An Adjective, when it is complementary to the Verbs **bi** and **is**, does not agree with its Noun, and is indeclinable. **Tha an oidhche dorch** *the night is dark,* **bu ghlan an gille e** *he was a handsome lad.*

It is so also with many Active Verbs when the Adjective is used complementary to the Verb, in which case it is very nearly an Adverb.

Rinn mi an sgian geur. *I made the knife (to be) sharp* or *I made-sharp the knife.*

Dh' fhàs a' bhean glic. *The woman grew (to be) wise* or *the woman grew-wise.*

Bhleith e a mhin mìn. *He ground the meal fine* or *he ground-fine the meal.*

It will be well to compare this construction with that in which the Adjective agrees with the Noun.

Rinn mi an sgian gheur. *I made the sharp knife.*
Dh' fhàs a' bhean ghlic. *The wise woman grew.*
Bhleith e a' mhin mhìn. *He ground the fine meal.*

ORDER.—The Adjective is usually placed after its Noun and next to it; **duine maith** *a good man,* **bean aoidheil** *an hospitable woman.*

The words **ro, gle, fior,** and indeed any word that rightly qualifies the Adjective may come between it and the Noun; **duine ro mhaith, bean fhior aoidheil, là anabarrach breagh** *an exceptionally fine day*—but such qualifying word is logically part of the Adjective always.

The Adjective with **bi** follows the Noun, with **is** it precedes the Noun; **tha an naigheachd maith** *the news is good,* **is maith an naigheachd** *that is good news = good is the news.*

A few Adjectives of one syllable are always put before their Noun; as, **droch each** *a bad horse,* **deagh mhisneach** *good courage.*

Some Adjectives may be placed before or after their Nouns; as, **gorm neul** or **neul gorm** *a dark-blue cloud,* **lag dhòchas** or **dòchas lag** *a feeble hope.* The usage which places the Adjective before the Noun is more poetical and pointed than the other, but the latter is always the order of simple prose. When Adjectives are thus put before the Noun there is a tendency for the two words to form a compound term, **gorm-neul, lag-dhochas.**

Numeral Adjectives whether Cardinal or Ordinal as well as kindred Adjectives like **iomadh** *many,* **gach** *every,* are placed before their Nouns; as, **tri laithean** *three days,* **an treas là** *the third day,* **iomadh duine** *many a man,* **gach eun gu a nead** *every bird to its nest.*

The exception usually made to this rule, namely, that the Adjective does not agree with the Noun in such expressions as **Righ Tearlach a h-Aon** *King Charles the First,* **Righ Seumas**

L

a **Cuig** *King James the Fifth*, does not seem to be commendable or necessary. It seems to be an imitation of English and even of that too much after the diction of Artemus Ward. The correct rendering of these expressions is, *King Charles (the) One* and *King James Five*, which is not sense. The Gaelic form should doubtless be **an ceud Righ Tearlach** *the First King Charles*, **an cuigeamh Righ Seumas** *the Fifth King James*.

A Compound Numeral like **aon-deug** *eleven*, **tri fichead 's a deich** *seventy*, takes the Noun after the first term of the compound form; as, **aon fhear deug** *eleven men*, **tri fichead fear 's a deich** *seventy men = threescore men and ten*. So the Ordinal also; **an t-aona fear deug** *the eleventh man*.

The Possessive Pronouns **mo**, **do** etc., are always placed before their Nouns; **mo lamh** *my hand*, **do chas** *thy foot*.

The Interrogatives **co, cia, ciod**, are placed before their Nouns with the Article intervening; **co am fear sin?** *who (is) that man?*

The Demonstratives **so, sin, sud**, when used as Adjectives follow the Noun; **na fir so** *these men* **na h-eoin sin** *those birds*, **na tighean ud** *yon houses*.

Of the Agreement of a Pronoun with its Antecedent

Personal and Possessive Pronouns agree with their antecedents in Number and Gender; **sheas a' bhean aig a chosaibh, agus thoisich i air am fliuchadh le a deuraibh, agus thiormaich i iad le folt a cinn** *the woman stood at his feet and she began to wet them with* *her tears, and she wiped them with the hair of her head.*

Except, Nouns for which the Gender and the Sex are not the same, in which the Pronoun agrees with the Sex and not with the Gender; **is maith an sgalag e** *he is a good farmservant.* In this instance the Sex is Masculine though the Noun is declined as a Feminine, hence the Pronoun in agreement is Masculine and not Feminine.

Akin to this are the following interesting examples; **an gobhlan-gaoithe mar an ceudn', do sholair nead dhi fein** *the swallow too hath provided a nest for herself.* **Gobhlan-gaoithe** is Masculine as appears by the Masculine Article, but as it is the dam that is spoken of, the reference is made by the Pronoun of the Feminine Gender.

So also '**Ta gliocas air a fireanachadh le a cloinn**' *Wisdom is justified by her children*, where **gliocas** is a Masculine Noun, but being here personified as a female, the Pronoun is adapted to that idea.

A Pronoun of which the antecedent is a Collective Noun is put in the Third Person Plural; **thoir àithne do 'n t-sluagh air eagal gu 'm bris iad a steach** *charge the people for fear they may break in.*

Two or more singular subjects require the Pronoun in the Plural; **chaidh Ian agus Lachann a shealg ach tillidh iad air an ais feasgar** *John and Lachlan went to hunt but they shall return in the evening.*

Nouns preceded by **gach, iomadh** though always Singular are often referred to by a Plural Pronoun; **chaidh gach duine gu an aite** *each* or *every man went to their place.*

When the Antecedent is a sentence or a clause, the Pronoun is in the Third Singular Masculine; **dh' ith na** bà caola na bà reamhra, agus cha 'n aithnichteadh orra e *the lean kine ate up the fat kine, and it could not be known on them.*

In an interrogative sentence involving an abstract and general conception, a Pronoun does not always agree with its Noun; **ciod e uirnigh** *what (is) it prayer?* But if the term be restricted or defined the Pronoun usually does agree; **ciod i Uirnigh an Tighearna** *what (is) it the Lord's Prayer?*

In an interrogative sentence including a Personal Pronoun and a Noun, as **co e am fear sin?** if the Noun be restricted in its signification by some other word or words (p. 161) the Pronoun usually follows (1) the Gender of the Noun, **co e am fear sin a theid suas** *who is the man that shall ascend?* or (2) the Sex of the Object signified by the Noun, **co i am boirionnach sin** *who is that woman?*—where, though **boirionnach** is Masculine in Gender it is Feminine in Sex, hence the Feminine Pronoun.

But if the Noun is not restricted the Pronoun is of the Masculine Gender **ciod e Uirnigh** *what is prayer?*

This is noticeable in **co dha a bhuineas e** *to whom belongs it?*

Of the Agreement of a Verb with its Nominative

As the Verb has no variation of FORM corresponding to the Person or Number of its Nominative, the connection between them can only be marked by their relative positions or their ORDER in the sentence.

The Nominative is always after, and next to the Verb except when enlargements of the Subject intervene; **tha mi** *I am*, **rugadh duine-cloinne** *a man-child is born*, **aithrisear iomadh droch sgeul** *many an evil tale is told.*

It should be noticed that, in the two sentences last given, the Verb of one is a Past Tense form **rugadh** used to express the Present, and that of the other is a Future Tense form **aithrisear** used for the same purpose (see p. 115).

In rhetorical sentences enlargements other than those of the Subject may intervene; **rugadh dhuinne, an diugh, ann am baile Dhaibhidh, an Slanuighear** *there is born to us, this day, in the city of David, the Saviour*; but the order **rugadh Slanuighear dhuinne an diugh** etc. is the correct Prose order.

The Prepositional Pronoun may with advantage be looked upon as the Indirect Object corresponding to the Latin Dative, **tha ubhlan againne** '*sunt nobis pōmă,*' *we have apples* = (*there*) *are apples at us*. It should be particularly observed that the *action* of the Verb must be in the same direction as, or consistent with the position indicated by, the Preposition; **thuit sin oirnn** *that fell upon us*, **chaidh neart asta** *strength went out of them*, **thig e chugam** *he shall come to me*. We cannot rightly say **thainig sin uainn** *that came from us*. Departure from this plain order and use of Prepositional Pronouns shall be referred to as Idioms.

In Poetry the Nominative may come before the Verb;

> **Gach doire, gach coire, 's gach eas**
> **Bheir 'am chuimhne cneas mo ghraidh**

Each grove, each dell, each waterfall will bring to my remembrance the form of my love.

In dramatic expression the Nominative may be omitted; **a Gharna cuim' a sheas? a Ghuill cuim' a thuit?** *Garno why stoodst? Gaul why didst fall?* This is a very rare construction.

The Infinitive may take the Nominative of the Agent before it, in which case the Preposition **do** is either expressed or understood before the Infinitive; **cha'n 'eil e iomchuidh sinne dh' fhàgail focail Dé, agus a fhrithealadh do bhordaibh** *it is not meet that we should leave the Word of God and serve tables* lit. *us to leave . . . and to serve*. The Preposition being softened as usual to a disappears after a Vowel, **air son mi bhi a ris maille ribh** *on account of my being (me to be) again present with you*—for **air son mi a bhi.**

The Relative Pronoun is always put before the Verb.

Of the Agreement of one Noun with another

When in the same sentence two or more Nouns, applied as names to the same object, stand in the same grammatical relation to other words, it should naturally be expected that their form, in so far as it depends on that Relation, should be the same; in other words, that Nouns denoting the same object, and related alike to the governing word, should agree in Case. This accordingly happens in Greek and Latin. In Gaelic, where a variety of form gives room for the application of the same rule, it has been followed in some instances; as, **Donnchadh mac Chailein mhic Dhomhnuill** *Duncan the son of Colin the son of Donald*, where the words **Chailein** and **mhic** denoting the same person, and being alike related to the preceding Noun **mac** are on that account both in the same Case. It must be acknowledged however, that this rule, obvious and natural as it is, has not been uniformly observed by the speakers of Gaelic. For example, instead of **mac Ioseiph an t-saoir** *the son of Joseph the carpenter* many would more readily say, **mac Ioseiph an saor**; instead of **thuit e le laimh Oscair an laoich chruadalaich** *he fell by the hand of Oscar the bold hero*, it would rather be said, **thuit e le laimh Oscair an laoch͜cruadalach.** The latter of these two modes of expression may perhaps be defended on the ground of its being elliptical; and the ellipsis may be supplied thus: **mac Ioseiph [is e sin] an saor; laimh Oscair [neach is e] an laoch cruadalach.** Still it must be allowed in favour of the rule in question, that the observance of it serves to mark the relation of the Nouns to each other, which would otherwise remain in many instances doubtful. Thus in one of the foregoing examples if we should reject the rule, and write **mac Ioseiph an saor**, it would be impossible to know, from the form of the words, whether Joseph or his son were the carpenter.

The translators of the Scriptures into Gaelic, induced probably by the reasonableness and utility of the rule under consideration, by the example of the most polished tongues, and by the usage of Gaelic itself in some phrases, have uniformly adhered to this rule when the leading Noun was in the Genitive; as, **do mhacaibh Bharsillai a' Ghileadaich**, 1 Kings ii. 7; **righ-chathair Dhaibhidh athar**, 1 Kings ii. 12; **do thaobh Bheniamin am brathar,** Judges xxi. 6; **ag gabhail nan clar cloiche, eadhon chlar a' cho-cheangail,** Deut. ix. 9.

This statement is taken in its entirety from Stewart and is retained though open to the following observations to which special attention is invited.

There can be no doubt that the practice of Gaelic is against the principle here laid down by Dr. Stewart for in the native and best usage, Nouns in apposition do not agree in Case. Apposition is expressed according to one or other of the following formulae.

1. **Dughall-taillear** *Dugald the tailor*, in which the two

Nouns conjoin and are declined together as a compound Noun, p. 61. This might be esteemed so far an Agreement.

2. **Ian Caimbeul am maor** *John Campbell the bailiff*, in which the first Noun consists of more than one word. **Ian Caimbeul** is declinable (as p. 61) but **am maor** is not. So, **tigh Iain Chaimbeil am maor** *the house of John Campbell the bailiff* —not **Iain Chaimbeil a' mhaoir**. In this there is no Agreement.

3. **Domhnall Camshron am maighstir-sgoil** *Donald Cameron the schoolmaster*, in which the Noun in apposition is a compound Noun, but undergoes no inflection. So, **tigh Dhomhnaill Chamshroin am maighstir-sgoil** *the house of Donald Cameron the schoolmaster*.

It may be stated briefly that excepting so much Agreement as is shown between the two Nouns as in the first example there is no Agreement between Gaelic Nouns in apposition—and, that the second Noun always retains the Nominative form.

All the confusion and discussion about this matter has arisen from a misunderstanding of the following construction.

Dughall an tailleir means *Dugald of the tailor*—some immediate dependant or a son of the tailor—and it does not mean *Dugald the tailor* as has been so often asserted. **An tailleir** is the regular Genitive governed by **Dughall** and is not the Nominative as those have thought who called it an apposition. It is not an Apposition.

If so much is clearly understood there can be no confusion in such an expression as **mac Ioseiph an saor**. If the expression were considered from the grammatical point of view alone, it might leave us in doubt as to the meaning, but usage is unequivocal and conclusive that it means and can only mean *the son of Joseph-the-carpenter.*

Even when the first Noun is Dative the Noun in Apposition remains in the Nominative **do a bhràithribh uile mic an righ** *to all his brothers the sons of the king.*

CHAPTER III—OF GOVERNMENT

Nouns

One Noun governs another in the Genitive; **ceann coin** *the head of a dog.*

The Noun governed is always placed after that which governs it, and this alone determines the Case of Nouns which have no distinct form for the Genitive—Nouns of First and Third Declension; **tobhta bàta** *the seat of a boat* i.e. the rower's seat; **balla tobhta** *a wall of turf.*

The Infinitives of Transitive Verbs being themselves Nouns (p. 115) govern in like manner the Genitive of their Object; **ag cur sil** *(at) sowing (of) seed,* **iar leughadh an t-soisgeil** *after reading (of) the Gospel.*

When the Noun governed does in its turn govern another Noun in the Genitive, the former is put in the Nominative instead of the Genitive Case; **de mheas craobhan a' ghàraidh**—not **chraobhan** *of the fruit of the trees of the garden,* **lamh bean-na-bainse**—not **mna-na-bainse** *the hand of the bride.*

The Infinitive also is so governed; **cuis crathadh cinn**

'us casadh béil—not **crathaidh, casaidh** *a cause of (for) shaking the head and curling the mouth,* **an deigh leughadh an lagha** *after reading of the law.*

If a compound term made up of a Noun and an Infinitive is followed by another Noun, the second term of the compound is in the Genitive; **tigh-bearraidh nam buachaillean** *the shearing-house of the shepherds.* In such an expression as **tigh-bearradh nan caorach** *the house for shearing of the sheep* in which the Infinitive remains in the Nominative, the hyphen and binding of the two words into a compound form is quite wrong. If there is to be any compounding it should be **tigh bearradh-nan-caorach**, for **bearradh nan caorach**—the whole Phrase—is an Adjective limiting the Noun **tigh**.

One Verb governs another in the Infinitive; **faodaidh mi bualadh** *I may strike* lit. *I am permitted striking* or *to strike*, **rinn mi eisdeachd** *I listened* lit. *I made listening.*

When the Infinitive form is used as a Noun it is governed in the Genitive by another Noun **aig deireadh fàis** *at the end of growing,* **a chum glaodhaich** *in order to call,* **a chum mo phòsaidh** *towards my wedding,* but when it is used with verbal signification it remains in the Nominative or uninflected form **faodaidh mi bualadh, feumaidh mi do bhualadh** *it is necessary for me to strike you,* **a chum am marbhadh** *in order to kill them* lit. *towards their killing.*

ADJECTIVES.—A few Adjectives signifying Fulness may govern a following Noun in the Genitive; **tigh làn òir** *a house full of gold,* **tha mi buidheach bidh** *I am satisfied with (of) food,* **còta làn tholl** *a coat full of* *holes.* This construction is by preference limited to Nouns signifying bulk or mass.

Adjectives expressive of Fulness or Want take **de** *of* after them—except the few Adjectives just mentioned, and these also take it if the Article precedes the Noun **làn de'n òr** *full of (the) gold*, **gann de stòras** *scant of wealth*, **sgìth de'n obair** *tired of the work.*

Adjectives expressive of Willingness, or their reverse, take the Infinitive after them **tha mi toileach toiseachadh** *I am willing to begin*, **cha'n'eil mi deonach do phòsadh** *I am not disposed to marry you.*

Adjectives expressive of Profit, Likeness, Proximity, etc. and their opposites take an appropriate Preposition after them—as in English; **mianach air urram** *desirous of (on) honour*, **maith air sgriobhadh** *good at writing*, **coltach ri 'athair** *like (to) his father*, **fagus do 'n tigh** *near to the house.*

VERBS.—A Verb Transitive governs its Object in the Accusative; **tog tigh** *raise a house*, **mharbh iad an righ** *they killed the king.*

Some Intransitive Verbs may take an Object of kindred meaning; **mun caidil thu cadal a' bhàis** *ere you sleep the sleep of (the) death.*

Many Transitive Verbs require a Preposition after them—as in English; **iarr air an duine tighinn** *ask the man to come*, **feoraich de'n ghille** *ask of the lad*, **leig-as mo lamh** *let go my hand.*

An Impersonal Verb takes **do** after it; **thuit domh bhì an Duneidin** *it fell to me to be in Edinburgh* = *it* *happened*, etc., **thachair dhomh tighinn** *it happened to me to come = it happened that I came,* **thig dhomh falbh** *it becomes me to go = it is time I went.*

Bu causes aspiration of a succeeding initial Consonant **bu mhaith sin** *that were well,* **bu chruaidh an càs** *hard was their case.*

Except Dentals; **bu dona sin** *that was bad,* **bu truagh an càs** *their case was pitiful.* The reason for this is in that **bu** has lost a terminal Dental. It used to be **bad, bud** and even **but** in its very early time.

PREPOSITIONS.—The Government of Prepositions has been referred to incidentally already.

All Prepositions govern the Dative;

Except (1) That **eadar** meaning *both* governs the Accusative (p. 125).

(2) That **gun** and **seach** always govern the Accusative (pp. 129, 134).

(3) That **gus** and **mar** govern the Accusative of a Noun preceded by the Article (pp. 127, 130).

And (4) that **tar** governs the Genitive (p. 125).

COMPOUND PREPOSITIONS govern the Noun following in the Genitive; **air feadh na tìre** *throughout the land,* **ré na h-ùine** *during the time,* but it is evident that this government follows on the fact that the governing word is a Noun.

Gu ruig governs the Accusative, but it is to be observed that the essential in this expression is a Verb (p. 147) and not a Noun as in the others.

A Preposition may govern a whole Phrase or Clause: **gus am bòrd a ghiulan** *to carry the table,* **luath chum fuil a dhòrtadh** *swift to shed blood.*

Eadar far an eirich grian
'Us far an luigh i siar 's a' chuan.

Idiomatic Construction

Considerable effort has failed to discover in the construction of the following idiomatic expressions any order that can be with advantage referred to the method and diction of English Grammar. The following arrangement may however be in some slight degree helpful. As the Prepositional Pronouns are the most troublesome elements, the classification is made with reference to them mainly. The idioms in **aig, air, do** and **le** are the most important :—

aig. **is mòr agam sin** *I value that greatly.*
tha deigh agam air *I desire it (him).*
tha cuimhne agam air *I remember him.*
tha tasdan agam air *he owes me a shilling.*
cha'n'eil agam air *I dislike him.*
chaidh agam air *I have overcome him.*
tha dòchas agam ann *I have hope in him—it.*
tha gràdh agam dha *I love him.*
tha truas agam dheth *I pity him.*
cha'n'eil omhail agam dha *he is no concern to me.*
tha bàigh agam ris *I feel kindly towards him.*
tha fiughair agam ris *I expect him.*

These may be taken as types, all the elements of which may change. Any appropriate part of the Verb may take the place of the part shown; **bu mhòr agam sin** *I did value that greatly*, **bidh cuimhne agam air** *I shall remember him*, **theid agam air** *I shall overcome him*; so with the Adjective or Noun following the Verb **is beag agam sin** *I value that (but) little*, **bha fuath agam dha** *I did hate him*; and with the other parts also **cha bu mhor air sud** *he did not value that (yon) much*, **tha bàigh aige rium** *he feels kindly towards me*.

air. is beag orm sin *I dislike that*, tha acras orm *I am hungry*.
    tha a' mhisg air, tha i air *he is drunk*.
    beir air *catch him*, dean tròcair orm *have pity on me*.
    eirich air *belabour him*, gabh air *thrash him*.
    dé tha cur ort *what ails thee*, tog ort *bestir thee*.
    thoir air labhairt *make him speak*.
    cha'n'eil air ach— *there is nothing for it but—*

do. is aithne dhomh sin *I know that*.
    is maith dhomh sin *that is well (good) for me*.
    is léir dhomh *I can see*, leig dhomh *permit me*.
    dé dh'eirich dhut *what has befallen thee?*
    nach ann domh a dh' eirich *to me what evil has befallen!*
    cha'n'eil dhomh ach— *all that is necessary for me is—*

le. is leam sin *that is mine*, is maith leam sin *that pleases me*.
    is coma leam sin *I dislike that* or *am indifferent to*.
    co leis an cù *whose is the dog?* tha e leam-sa *it is mine*.
    shaoil leam *I thought, surmised*, theid leam *I will prosper*.
    leam fein *alone*, ge b'oil leam *in spite of me*.

others. tha mi 'nam shaor *I am a carpenter*, 'nam chadal *asleep*
    thug iad an car asam *they cheated me*.
    tha mi mòr as *I am proud of him*.
    tha iad as mo dheigh *they are after me*.
    tog dheth *give it up*, thainig sin fodham *I was so disposed*.

cha d' thainig sin rium *that did not agree with me.*
tha iad rium *they are 'at me,'* leig ris sin *show that.*
tha mi fo churam uime *I am anxious about him.*

The Adverbial usage of the Prepositional Pronouns has been already referred to. It should be observed in this connection specially; **fhuair e dheth** *he got off,* **chuir iad chuige mi** *they have forced me,* **chaidh iad as** *they have gone (out),* **chaidh iad thairis** *they went across,* **theid a' ghrian fodha** *the sun will go down,* **thoir seachad sin** *give that over.*

It will be a most profitable and interesting exercise to alter the terms in these expressions—and to observe the change in meaning.

NOTE.—REGULAR VERB AND PARTICLES
(*Refer page* 102)

There are only a few essential forms of the regular Verb:

I. The STEM—**buail, òl.**

It takes **na** to form a Negative **na buail** *strike not.*

II. The FUTURE INDICATIVE—**buailidh, òlaidh.**

It takes no Particle.

III. The PAST SUBJUNCTIVE—**bhuailinn, bhuaileadh.**

It may take all Particles. It is Aspirated with **ged, ma, o'n** but not with the others **ged bhuailinn** *though I would strike* but **mur buailinn** *if I would not strike,* **nach buaileadh tu** *would you not strike?*

IV. The FUTURE SUBJUNCTIVE—**bhuaileas.**

It always follows **ged, ma o'n**; as, **ma bhuaileas mi** *if I shall strike,* **ma dh' òlas mi** *if I shall drink.*

The Past Indicative is formed from the Stem by Aspiration after (do); as, (do) bhuail, dh' òl.

It takes all Particles. Negatives and Interrogatives and **na 'n** restore **do**; as, **mur do bhuail mi** *if I did not strike*, **nach d' òl mi** *did I not strike?* Conditionals do not take **do** before Consonants **ged bhuail mi** *though I struck* but that it has only dropped is shown by its appearing before vowels **ma dh' òl mi** *if I drank* in which position it gets Aspirated, being vowel-flanked.

It will be observed that the Tenses of the Negative-Interrogative Mood are merely formed from the Past Indicative and the Stem by Interrogative and Negative Particles, and that—excepting the Verb **bi**—this Mood has no forms of its own.

List of Works on Celtic Antiquity

PUBLISHED OR SOLD BY

DAVID NUTT, 270-271 STRAND, LONDON.

GRIMM LIBRARY No. 4.

The Voyage of Bran, Son of Febal, to the Land of the Living. An Old Irish Saga now first edited, with Translation, Notes, and Glossary. By KUNO MEYER.

With an Essay upon the Irish Vision of the Happy Otherworld and the Celtic Doctrine of Rebirth. By ALFRED NUTT. Section I: THE HAPPY OTHERWORLD. Crown 8vo. xvii + 330 pp. Printed on laid paper. Cloth, uncut. 10s. 6d. net.

MONSIEUR HENRY GAIDOZ in *Mélusine*.—'Edition, tradition et commentaire philologique sont d'une critique irréprochable, et telle qu'on pourrait les attendre de M. Kuno Meyer, un des meilleurs irlandistes de notre temps. . . . M. Nutt a précédé avec beaucoup de critique et de clarté : il n'a pas, comme font tant d'écrivains, melé sans ordre les analogies de toutes provenance . . . le tableau est tracé d'une main sure : M. Nutt est bien informé: ses matériaux sont pris aux meilleures sources : son exposition est nette et précise : son livre est une œuvre d'histoire générale à la fois des croyances et des littératures.'

By PROFESSOR KUNO MEYER.

The Vision of Mac Conglinne. Irish Text, English Translation (revision of Hennessy's), Notes, and Literary Introduction. Crown 8vo. 1892. liv + 212 pp. Cloth. 10s. 6d.

One of the curious and interesting remains of mediæval Irish story-telling. A most vigorous and spirited Rabelaisian tale, of equal value to the student of literature or Irish legend.

Merugud Uilix Maicc Leirtis. The Irish Odyssey. Edited, with Notes, Translation, and a Glossary. 8vo. 1886. xii + 36 pp. Cloth. Printed on handmade paper, with wide margins. 3s.

By WHITLEY STOKES, LL.D.

Cormac's Glossary. Translated and Annotated by JOHN O'DONOVAN. Edited, with Notes and Indices, by W. S. 1868. 4to. Calcutta.

The few remaining copies of this scarce and valuable work can be procured from D. Nutt, at £1, 10s. net.

On the Calendar of Oengus. Comprising Text, Translation, Glossarial Index, Notes. 4to. 1880. xxxi + 552 pp. 18s. net.

The Bodley Dinnshenchas. Edited, Translated, and Annotated. 8vo. 1892. 2s. 6d. net.

The Edinburgh Dinnshenchas. Edited, Translated, and Annotated. 8vo. 1893. 2s. 6d. net.

The Dinnshenchas is an eleventh-century collection of topographical legends, and one of the most valuable and authentic memorials of Irish mythology and legend. These two publications give nearly three-fourths of the collection as preserved in Irish MSS. The bulk of the Dinnshenchas has never been published before, either in Irish or in English.

Waifs and Strays of Celtic Tradition

ARGYLLSHIRE SERIES.

VOL. I.

Craignish Tales. Collected by the Rev. J. MacDougall; and Notes on the War Dress of the Celts by Lord Archibald Campbell. xvi+98 pp. 20 plates. 1889. 5s. net.

VOL. II.

Folk and Hero Tales. Collected, Edited (in Gaelic), and Translated by the Rev. D. Macinnes: with a Study on the Development of the Ossianic Saga, and copious Notes by Alfred Nutt. xxiv+497 pp. Portrait of Campbell of Islay, and Two Illustrations by E. Griset. 1890. 15s.

VOL. III.

Folk and Hero Tales. Collected, Edited (in Gaelic), Translated, and Annotated by the Rev. J. MacDougall; with an Introduction by Alfred Nutt, and Three Illustrations by E. Griset. 330 pp. 1892. 10s. 6d.

VOL. IV.

The Fians: West Highland Traditions of Fionn Mac Cumhail and the Fians. Collected during the past forty years. Edited (in Gaelic) and Translated by the Rev. J. G. Campbell of Tiree; with Introduction and Bibliographical Notes by Alfred Nutt. 8vo. 300 pp. 1892. 10s. 6d.

VOL. V.

Clan Traditions and Popular Tales of the Western Highlands and Islands. Selected from the papers of the late Rev. J. G. Campbell of Tiree. With Memoir and Portrait of Author. 8vo. 250 pp. 1895. 5s. 6d.

Beside the Fire: Irish Gaelic Folk Stories. Collected, Edited, Translated, and Annotated by Douglas Hyde, M.A.; with Additional Notes by Alfred Nutt. 8vo. lviii+203 pp. Cloth. 7s. 6d.

The Irish printed in Irish character.

By ALFRED NUTT.

Studies on the Legend of the Holy Grail. With Especial Reference to the Hypothesis of its Celtic Origin. Demy 8vo. xv+281 pp. Cloth. 10s. 6d. net.

'Une des contributions les plus précieuses et les plus méritoires qu'on ait encore apportées à l'éclaircissement de ces questions difficiles et compliquées.'—Mons. Gaston Paris in *Romania*.

The Buddha's Alms-Dish and the Legend of the Holy Grail. (*Archæological Review*, June 1889.) 2s. 6d.

www.ingramcontent.com/pod-product-compliance
Lightning Source LLC
Chambersburg PA
CBHW032142160426
43197CB00008B/748